The Affinity Photo Guidebook

A Step-by-Step New User's Manual

Frank Walters

- 2nd Edition -

We are a self-publishing company employing several authors. We take our books very seriously and try our very best to publish high-quality books that deliver the expected results we advertise in our book descriptions. If there is ever an issue with syntax, content or book layout, please don't hesitate to contact us before you leave negative comments. We promise we will address your concerns as quickly as we can. Software develops quickly and when we publish our books we know in a short time there will be new updates. We promise to try to keep up with updates in all of our books as the software updates.

For permissions, questions or to submit your own artwork, contact us at **KuhlmanPublishing@yahoo.com**

ISBN: 979-8838-3909-05

- 2nd Edition -

As of July 2022, we have gone through all of our lessons to make sure they work as they are shown in this book. We have also uploaded all of the images to our Facebook page where we'll provide you a direct link to be able to download all of the images for this book.

Dedication

This book is dedicated to you, our readers. Thank you for the many times you have emailed us to ask for the various image folders and to ask for specific questions regarding the lessons we teach.

We love to interact with all of you. It's the whole reason we started writing these books - to reach out to you and help you learn how to work with Affinity Photo.

So, thank you for purchasing our book(s) and for communicating with us how we can better serve you.

Best regards,
Charles & Frank

Unique Offer

Have you ever wanted your name in print? If so, then we have a deal for you. Find anything wrong inside this book like spelling, punctuation, or even a skill step that no longer works, and we'll add your own name to this Dedication page. It's our special way of saying "Thank you" for helping us make better books.

Readers who have helped us create a better book.

1. Bill Oldham - Australia

2.

Examples of Techniques You'll Learn

Double Exposure Effect

How to Create Realistic Shadows

Impressive 3D Pop-Out Effects

Water Flame Candles (p. 125)

Transparent Text Effects

Who is this book for?

This book is specifically written for ***beginners*** of Affinity Photo and those curious about how to use this awesome software.

If you are a professional photo editor, then this book will be too basic for you. If you're coming from the Adobe architecture of programs, then this book is a good starting guide for you as an introduction to the Affinity architecture of programs.

How is the book structured?

We'll guide you through the first 10 basic skills new users need to learn how to use when starting out with Affinity Photo. Then, we'll continue teaching you how to do 20 interesting techniques in our unique step-by-step method.

What makes our teaching style unique?

We try to boil every step down to its most basic form so that complicated steps become simple. We pride ourselves in trying to take a complex effect and make it accessible to anyone.

We also use our own method of italicizing action words and bolding objective words. This makes it very clear what you should do. For example: *Press* the **Refine** button and then *press* **OK**.

The Step-by-Step Instructions

One of the criticisms we receive is the fact that new users have hard time following the instructions exactly how we have them laid out. Unfortunately, photo editing is a precise art. Each step builds upon the next. If you skip one step, the entire project won't work. Trust us, we wish it was otherwise, but it's not.

Contact us if you ever get frustrated and we promise we'll respond as fast as we can to help you out of any jamb you might find yourself in. We are here for you 100%.

Image Quality

Amazon is our publisher and printer. If you have concerns about the quality of the images in our book(s), please do not leave a negative review. We have nothing to do with the printing process. In most cases, you can return the book if you are not happy with it.

A Note about Redundancy

Learning new skills take a lot of repetition. We know this, so we structured this book with lots of the same ideas and shortcuts. This is done so you learn as fast as possible. We'll consider we've done our job if when you are done going through this book, you're able to retain most of the skills you learnt in this book.

Download the Images First Before You Start

We only use license-free images we find on Pixabay, Unsplash, and Pexels. Before you start working in this book, you'll need to download all of the images for this book and place them in a folder on your Desktop named "Affinity Photo Guidebook" (or another name you like better).

You can do these two ways:

1. Contact us and we'll email you the image folder and give you a free gift (see below).

2. Go to our Facebook page and download the images from there.

Our email is **kuhlmanpublishing@yahoo.com**

Our Facebook page is: **https://www.facebook.com/WritePublish/**

To find the images on our Facebook homepage, *click* where is reads **Photos** and then *click* where you see the name of this book - **The Affinity Photo Guidebook**.

Positive Reviews

Positive reviews really make a difference! It shows our writers that they are doing a good job. If there is anything you don't like about our book, please contact us at **kuhlmanpublishing@yahoo.com** and we promise we'll help you as fast as we can or address the situation you are not in favor with.

Intro: The Eight Areas of the Affinity Photo Screen

Every new software has its own screen set-up. Affinity Photo is no different. To make your learning as easy as possible, we have divided the User Interface (UI) screen up into eight different areas. You can also find a detailed graphic in Basics 2 that will visually show you where all of these areas are on the screen.

It's very important to know exactly where each of these areas are located. During the course of this book, we'll give you prompts like:

Go to the **Menu bar** - **File** - **Save...** and you'll have to know what that means.

It means simply: Go to the top of the screen where the Menu bar is located and click on File. This will open a drop-down menu where we want you to click on the option Save...

The eight areas of the screen are:

Area 1: Tools

Located vertically on the far-left side of the screen below and to the left of the Contextual Toolbar. This is where all the tools are located.

Area 2: Menu bar

Located at the very top of the screen - including File, Edit, Text, Document, Layers, Select, Arrange, Filters, View, Window, Help.

Area 3: Toolbar

Parallel line directly under the **Menu bar** - from L to R it starts to the right of the **Photo Persona** icon and extends all the way to the right to an icon which looks like a **white** circle with its bottom right quarter in **blue** (or **Insert inside the selection**).

Area 4: Contextual Toolbar

Running parallel and directly below the Toolbar. These options change depending on which tool you choose. Click on some of the different Tools to see the Contextual Toolbar change.

Area 5: Studios / Panels

The studios are located on the far right-side of the screen.

Area 6: Icons bar

Located under the Layers Panel, this is where all of the useful icons are located like the Mask Layer, Adjustments, Live Filters, New Pixel Layer, and the Trashcan. We refer very often to this area.

Area 7: Document / Image

The document is found in the middle of the screen, and it is the item (document, illustration, photo) you are currently working on.

Area 8: Canvas

This is the area in the middle of the screen surrounding the document.

The Most Common Shortcuts You Need to Know

To maximize your proficiency in using this software, we highly recommend you learn the shortcuts most often used. Knowing these will greatly increase your performance and speed. While there are many more to learn, these here are the ones you'll use the most. The "+" used below is not to be pressed, except when zooming in & out (to Undo, you will *press* **Ctrl/Cmd Z,** but we added the "+" to just show that in addition to *pressing* **Ctrl/Cmd** you also need to *press* **Z** at the same time).

There are many other shortcuts you'll learn along the way, but these are the main ones you'll need to know.

Windows Users:	Use **Ctrl** (not **Cmd**)	**Zoom in**	**Ctrl/Cmd +**
Mac Users:	Use **Cmd** (not **Ctrl**)	**Zoom out**	**Ctrl/Cmd –**
		Invert	**Ctrl/Cmd+I**
Undo	**Ctrl/Cmd+Z**	**Duplicate**	**Ctrl/Cmd+J**
Redo	**Ctrl/Cmd+Y**	**Deselect**	**Ctrl/Cmd+D**
Copy	**Ctrl/Cmd+C**	**Select All**	**Ctrl/Cmd+A**
Paste	**Ctrl/Cmd+V**		
Cut	**Ctrl/Cmd+X**	**Invert Pixel Selection**	**Ctrl/Cmd+Shift+I**

Test Yourself

(Check your own answers)

Write down the shortcut for.

1. Duplicate _____
2. Undo _____
3. Copy _____
4. Paste _____

Write down the action for these shortcuts (opposite from above questions).

1. Ctrl/Cmd+D_____

2. Ctrl/Cmd - _____

3. Ctrl/Cmd+V_____

4. Ctrl/Cmd+I _____

Table of Contents

First 10 Skills for Beginners

In this first section, we will be covering the basics of Affinity Photo. Please make sure you are familiar with these first 10 skills so that you will be able to apply what you will learn to the 20 tutorials that follow. You will probably refer back to these pages often. Repetition is the best teacher.

Again, be sure to have downloaded all of the images from the preceding pages into a specific Affinity Photo folder on your desktop. Doing this will save you very much time.

Basics 1 – How to Open Images/Documents/Templates

In Affinity Photo there are several ways to open Images onto the canvas. We'll discuss how to Open Documents and Templates after we've explained how to open images.

To open images, there are 5 ways to do this:

1. Open...

Go to the **Menu bar** - **File** - **Open** (or use the shortcut **Ctrl/Cmd+O**). This will open up your computer's search pop-out window where you can choose from which folder or location the image you want is located and then when you find it, *double-click* on the **image file** and it will be opened into the Affinity Photo screen.

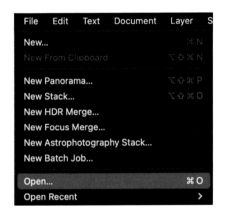

2. Open Recent

This will open a recently opened image that you may or may not have used with Affinity Photo. This is a useful option for when you need to work with multiple images over several hours.

3. Open... RAW Image

Opening images that are in RAW format will be immediately placed in the Develop Persona where you can make edits to the image before you upload it as a regular photo image (.jpg or .png). You do not need to specify that you have a RAW image, Affinity Photo will know automatically.

4. Stock Images

Affinity Photo lets you locate stock images directly inside the UI so that once you find an image you want to edit, you simply *click* on that **image** & *drag* it onto the canvas. There is a Stock tab located directly under the Color Wheel in the Layers Studio (see black rectangle). In order to *drag, drop* & *release* a stock photo (see yellow arrow), you need to first have an open document on the canvas.

Affinity Photo has three websites where you can use their Stock photography. Simply *click* on the vertical double-arrows (see our yellow rectangle) to *choose* between Unsplash, Pexels, and Pixabay. First *type* in the title of the image you are looking for (we typed "model").

5. *Click & Drag*

Click & *drag* also works. Simply *click* on an **image** someplace on your computer & *drag* it onto the Affinity Photo canvas. Be sure when doing this, be sure to place the new image and release it on a blank area of the canvas. That will cause it to be its own image separate from an existing image (if there is one already on the canvas). If you *click* & *drag* an image from your computer and release the mouse button over an existing image, the new image will become part of the underlying image. If this happens, simply *press* **Crtl/Cmd+Z** to *undo* your action. Then, go back and do it properly.

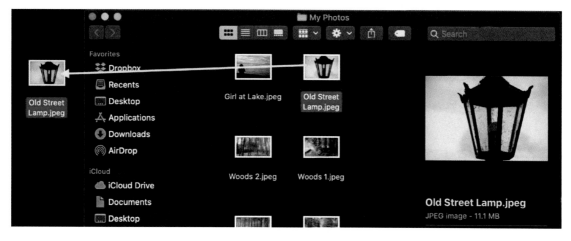

6. Open with...

Find an image on your computer and *right-click* on it and in the pop-out window choose Affinity Photo.

7. New... (Document)

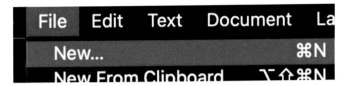

When you *click* on **New...** (**Ctrl/Cmd+N**), a pop-out window will appear where you can choose which form of Document you want to use: A **Preset** or a **Template** (see left-side of image below).

See **Basics #9** for a full tutorial on opening new Documents and creating Presets.

First, let's discuss the Presets - There are seven categories: My Presets, Print, Print Ready, Photo, Web, Devices, Architectural.

Note: The right-side of the screen, the **Layout**, is where you can change your particularly sized document's dimensions and DPI. Once you find a preset you like and want to keep it for later, *click* on the "circled+" (see yellow rectangle) at the top of the Layout area and it'll become a new Preset.

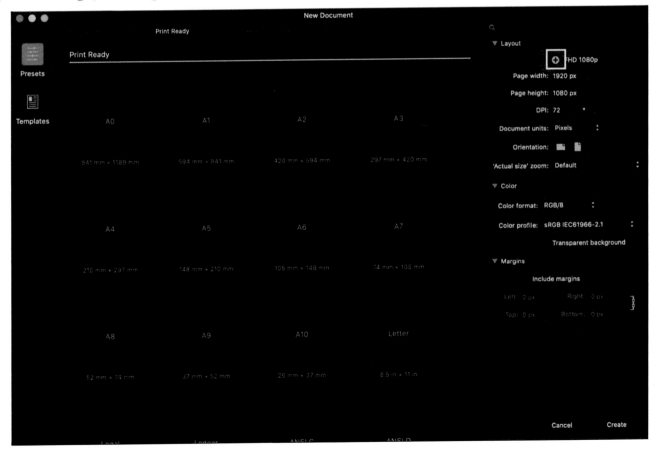

My Presets is where you'll place the specifically sized documents you use all the time. This will be your go-to category for most of our new documents.

Print & **Print Ready** handle documents you print. **Print Ready** is calibrated for specific printers.

Photo is for photos of different sizes. This is useful when you need a specific print size.

Devices is to be used when you need to make sure your document fits perfectly within a specific device's screen.

Architectural is a preset to be used for architecture images.

Templates: These are pre-made items containing images, layers, effects, and other settings all pre-prepared for you to use. You can make your own templates or you can probably find a few freebees online.

Done. This ends this lesson.

Write down ten things you want to learn how to do / or get clarity on:

1.

2.

3.

4.

5.

6.

7.

8.

9.

10.

A funny offer by the publisher

If you find any errors in this book and email us and tell us what it is, we'll edit the book with your corrections and add your name on the Dedications page so your name will be in print for all time. It's the least we can offer you if you help us make our books better by finding errors or misspellings.

So far, Bill Oldham from Australia has been included in our Dedications list.

Finished. This ends this tutorial.

Basics 2 – Affinity Photo's User Interface (aka the Screen)

The 2nd skill to learn is understanding how the Affinity Photo`s User Interface (UI) is organized. In this book we simply call everything you see "the screen".

There are eight different parts of the screen you need to be aware of. These are:

1. Tools
2. Menu bar
3. Toolbar
4. Contextual Toolbar

5. Studios / Panels
6. Icons bar
7. Document / Image
8. Canvas

On the left side of the screen are all the **Tools** you need to edit your pictures.

Whenever you *click* on the **Tools**, different options appear at the top of the interface. This top section above the canvas and on top of the image tabs is called the Contextual Toolbar.

The Contextual Toolbar allows you to make different changes, like *changing* the **Width** of the **Brush**, or *adjust* the level of an image's **Opacity**.

On the right-side of the screen's interface, you have the **Studios**. At the top of the **Studios**, you can *click* on **Color**, **Histogram** (Hgm), **Swatches** (Swt), **Brushes**, and **Macro** and in the middle section of the **Studio**, you have different panels –**Adjustment, Layers, Effects, Styles, Stock.**

Here is how to use some of these panels and some of the tools.

To **Add/Delete** Studio panels:

Go to the **Menu bar** and *choose* **View**

Select **Studio** from the drop-down menu.

Check **on** the panels you want to ***add***.

Check **off** the panels you want to ***delete***.

Note: In this image, **Adjustments** are added while **Assets** are not added to the Studios.

To *reset* the **Studio** options (this is important to remember if you accidently *press* the **wrong buttons** in the Studio):

Go to the **Menu bar** and *choose* **View**.

Select **Studio** from the drop-down menu.

Click **Reset Studio** (this is located at the very bottom of the list).

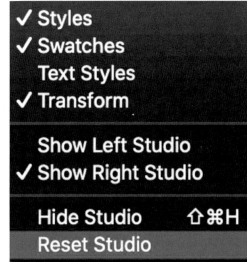

Affinity Photo can customize its tools from the left side panel.

To do this:

Go to the **Menu bar** and *choose* **View**.

Select **Customize Tools** (watch for a pop-out window).

Use *drag* & *drop* to *move* any **Tools** you want to add to the left-side column. You can also do the opposite and remove any Tool from the left-side Tool column and place it back in the pop-out window full of tools by *click* & *drag* if you want to.

For example, you can take the **Red Eye Removal Tool** and *drag* it to the Tools column (yellow arrow).

Special Note:

The most important thing we can recommend to you is to change the Tools column from one to two columns. Why? Because with two columns, the Fore-/Background colors will be placed at the bottom of the Tools. This is extremely helpful as you increase in your mastery of this program.

To do this:

Go to the **Number of Columns** tab on the bottom left-hand portion of the pop-out window and *select* the number of the columns that you prefer (e.g. 2).

You will now have two columns of **Tools** on the left-side of the UI with the Fore-/Background color circles present as well.

When you're done with customizing your **Tools**, *press* **Close** (see image to the right).

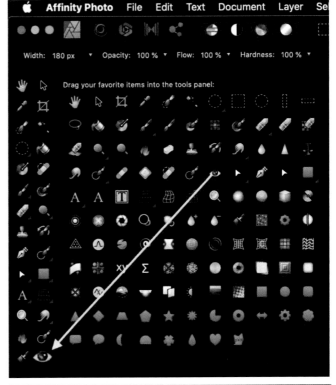

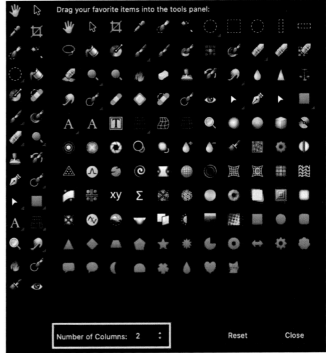

To *reset* the settings of the **Toolbar**, *click* the **Reset button** in the bottom right-hand corner next to Close.

The Personas

The different Personas are located on the top left-side of the screen. Each Persona has its own Tools, Studios/Panels. As you become more familiar with Affinity Photo, you'll be changing Personas to match your job. 95% of the time, you will probably work in the Photo Persona.

Personas = Workspaces

You'll do most of your work using **Photo Persona.**

Here are the five different types:

1. **Photo Persona**: This is the persona you will use the most for editing, cropping, making selections, using brushes, retouching, etc.

2. **Liquify Persona**: Used primarily to distort images.

3. **Develop Persona**: Used primarily for RAW images (i.e., when you upload a RAW file, it will automatically be opened into this Persona.

4. **Tone Mapping Persona**: Used for Tone Mapping.

5. **Export Persona**: Used to export in different formats.

Finished. This ends this tutorial.

Basics 3 – How to Crop Pictures

The third skill new users want to learn is how to crop images. Most of us have cropped many photos in our lifetimes using smartphones or digital cameras, so this won't be a hard lesson to understand or follow along. That being said, we think there will be some new things you'll learn in this lesson - Affinity Photo does have some cool tricks up its sleeves. Before we get started, please have this image uploaded to your screen: **Basics 3 - Crop**. If you'd prefer to use the hyperlink to find the photo, here it is:

https://pixabay.com/photos/sky-sunset-darwin-sunset-sky-2910164/

Ready to start?

With the image open on your screen, let's learn how to crop.

Select the **Crop Tool** (or *press* **C**).

Click on the **nodes** located on the image's perimeter & *move* **them** however you want to create the cropped image you need. We usually use one of the four corners of the crop square.

Press **Apply** when done (you can also simply *press* **Enter** on your keyboard).

Note: After you crop your picture, Affinity Photo keeps the original (see grey area around out cropped portion of the photo). To see where your original image was before you performed the crop, *select* the **Move Tool** (or *press* **V**) and you'll see the original image's perimeter. This image shows the middle-cropped area we selected as well as the part of the original we are excluding.

If you want to recapture some of the original image from the crop:

Select the **Crop Tool** (or *press* **C**).

Move the **squares** to left/right/up/down until you have your original photo back.

Press **Enter** (or *click* on **Apply**).

Another great feature of the **Crop Tool** is that it allows you to straighten crooked horizons.

To do this:

Select the **Crop Tool** (or *press* **C**).

Press the **Straighten button** in the middle of the Contextual Toolbar.

Click & *drag* on the **part of your picture** that you want ***straightened***. Look at the left image below where we placed the line on the horizon we want to straighten. As you do this, you will be drawing a white line (see the top of **Before** image).

Release you **mouse button** and the horizon you indicated will be made straight (see **After** image).

Before

After

To *rotate* your **picture** while in Crop mode:

Click with your mouse **someplace outside the image** (creating a 2-arrow cursor). Unfortunately, we are unable to make a screenshot of this 2-arrow cursor to show you).

Click & *drag* to **rotate** the photo.

Press **Enter** to confirm the rotation.

To remove the transparent area which appeared after straightened the horizon, we need to crop the image again and crop out this transparent area.

Done. This is our final image.

Finished. This ends this tutorial.

Basics 4 – How to Remove Imperfections from a Photo

The 4th skill beginners want to learn is how to remove unwanted objects or imperfections from a photo. For us, these two effects are still in the magical category. It just blows our mind that after a photo has been taken, we can go inside Affinity Photo and with a click of a button whatever we've selected not only disappears as if it never was, but the software hides the removed object perfectly. Just amazing!

The images we'll be using for this lesson are titled **Basics 4 -Kid** and **Basics 3 - Face**. Please have the first one uploaded to your screen so we can start the lesson. Here is its hyperlink.

https://www.facebook.com/WritePublish/photos/a.351772392040734/1136837470200885

In this example, we're going to remove the poles sticking out of the water.

Before we start, we want to *duplicate* the **image** by *pressing* **Ctrl/Cmd+J.**

Now we have two copies of the picture. The reason we do this is because we work non-destructively – this will keep the original image safe by working on a copy of it.

Before we start this tutorial, we want to learn a little about working non-destructively. This is a very important part of photo-editing software that we want to briefly discuss this. We will restart the tutorial on the next page.

If you look at the Layers Panel, you will see that there are two **Background** layers. The layer on the very bottom is the original image. Looking at these layers you might be able to understand how affecting changes on the above **Background** layer doesn't destroy or touch the lowest **Background** image.

You can also tell which is the original image by the **Lock icon** on the right-side of its layer.

Do you understand what it means to work destructively (the opposite of non-destructive)? It means you are working on your original image and making changes to it. When you go to save the image, your original will be lost and, in a sense, "destroyed".

Therefore, whenever you are working with original images that you don't want to be ruined, you should always *duplicate* the **original** by *pressing* **Ctrl/Cmd+J.** This shortcut will make a **duplicate** copy of your original so that when you add layers (Adjustments, paintings, other images) on top of the duplicated image, your original will not be touched.

This piece of advice is especially important for users who edit RAW images.

This knowledge is very important. We hope you understand its importance. If you need further clarification, we are sure you can do a Google search and read all about "non-destructive image editing".

Now that we have a better understanding of what it means to work non-destructively, let's get back to this important tutorial

After duplicating the image, let's remove the metal poles from the water.

To do this:

Select the **Inpainting Brush Tool** (it looks like a brush with a circle at its tip). Inpainting is smart content removal.

Go to the **Contextual Toolbar** and *change* the **Brush's Width** so its circular brush stroke is a little wider than the wooden post in the bottom right corner of the photo. For us it is 100 px.

Paint over an **imperfection** (the poles in the lower right-hand corner) & Affinity Photo will remove them.

If you want to see before & after, *turn* off the **duplicate** image that you made earlier in this example:

Go to the **Layers Panel**.

Check the **duplicate** picture *off* & *on*.

Note: If you look closely at the two preview thumbnails (the small square images on the left-side of each layer) on both layers, you'll see that the top layer does not have the poles, but the lower layer does. So, when we uncheck (or deactivate) the top layer the poles return. This is because we are only seeing the bottom layer.

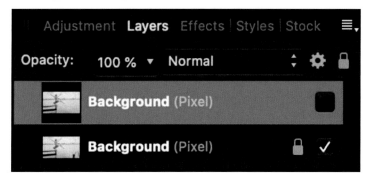

Part 2 of **Removing Imperfections**

For this example, you should be working with the image of a man's face. Ezra is the founder of Affinity Revolution. It is from his lessons that we got our start in Affinity Photo. We recommend his online courses.

Here is the hyperlink for this image:

https://www.facebook.com/WritePublish/photos/a.351772392040734/1136838333534132

Here, we are going to use the same tool, the **Inpainting Brush Tool**, but for removing some facial imperfections.

To do this:

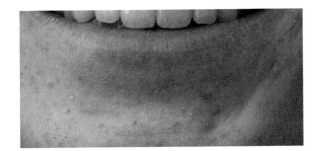

Press **Ctrl/Cmd+J** to *duplicate* the **image**.

Press **Ctrl/Cmd+** to *zoom in* to the **man's face**.

Hold-down the **Space bar** and *click* on the **image** & *drag* it **around the canvas** to your perfect position.

Click again on the **Inpainting Brush Tool** so it's activated.

Go to the **Contextual Toolbar** and *make* **these changes** to the Brush:

Change the **Hardness** to **100%**.

Change the **Width** to the about half the size of on one of the two front teeth. The width of the brush is a personal choice. Personally, when we use the Selection Brush Tool, we try to keep the width of the brush just a little bit bigger than the point on the image we are going to be altering.

In this example, we are working with very small imperfections, so a small brush size should be used.

Note: When *adjusting* the different tool measurements (like Width, Opacity, Flow, Hardness, etc.), there are two ways to increase or decrease their values (or the %). This is not our Width setting.

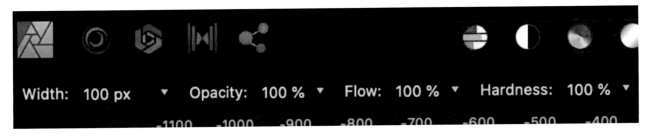

First, *double-click* the **window** and *type* in the **number** you want (in this case we typed **100**).

Second, you can *click* on the **downward-pointing diamonds** located to the right of the % symbol and a slider will appear (see yellow squares). Then you'll *slide* to the left for a smaller amount or to the right for a larger amount.

Now we're ready to use our brush to remove the imperfections we find on the man's face.

Click & *drag* the **red-tinted cursor** over the area you want to fix.

Release the **button** & the software will *remove* the **imperfection** (just like when we used this tool to remove the poles in the jumping image before.

These are the areas we corrected. For this tutorial, we made the Opacity for these red marks 50% so you could see the underlying acne for reference.

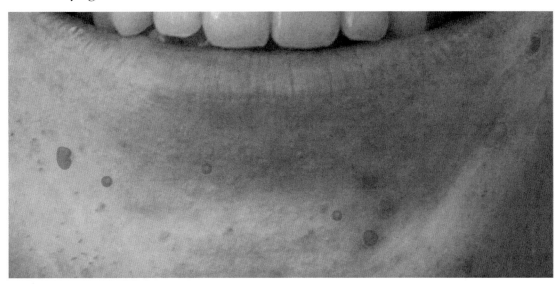

This is the image after these edits.

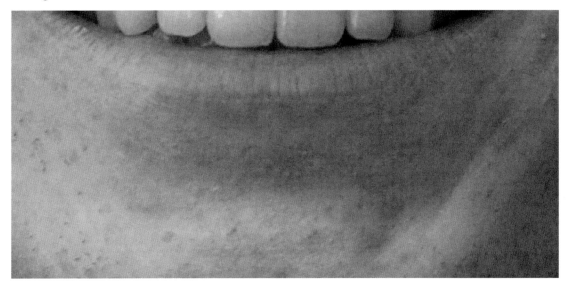

Uncheck the **top layer** in the Layers Panel to see ***before*** & ***after***.

If you are not happy with the result, you can repeat the steps above for removing imperfections until you get the perfect view for your image.

Finished. This ends this tutorial.

Basics 5 – How to Use the Adjustments Layer

The 5th skill beginners want to know is how to use Adjustment layers. It's probably the most fundamental skill new users need to know, and, in this lesson, you'll have the chance to use three popular adjustment layers: Black and White, Brightness & Contrast, and HSL.

This lesson will show you the basics of using adjustment layers. Here is the name of the image we'll be using for this lesson. **Basics 5/6 - Seashells.** Please have it uploaded to your screen so we can start. Here is the current hyperlink to this image: **https://pixabay.com/photos/seashell-shell-shells-sea-ocean-2821388/**

Before we start the lesson, let's talk about what adjustment layers are. Adjustment layers are layers that we place on top of the image layer we're working on. Since Adjustment layers stack on top, and are not a part of the image layer, they can be altered, moved, turned *off* & *on*, and deleted. Because they do not directly affect the original image, they are considered non-destructive.

Ready to start? To apply an **Adjustment** layer:

Go to the **icons bar** and *click* on the **Adjustments icon** (see yellow square - it's kinda hidden).

Select **Black and White...** from the drop-down menu.

This will make the picture become **black & white**.

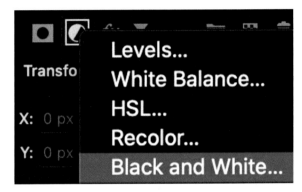

Note: Every adjustment layer works differently. In this case, we can use the sliders in the pop-out window to determine how bright and dark certain colors become in our **black & white** picture.

For example, if we *move* the **Red** slider to the **left**, our **red** colors on the picture will become **darker**.

But, if we move it to **right**, the **reds** will become **lighter**.

In this example the picture looks better with **darker**, so let`s move it back to the **left**.

Adjust the **Red** slider to **23%**.

Adjust the **Cyan** to **-17%**.

Continue the process with any of the sliders you'd like to change to make your learning more personal.

Press the **red button** at the top-left of this pop-out window to close (see this image for the red button).

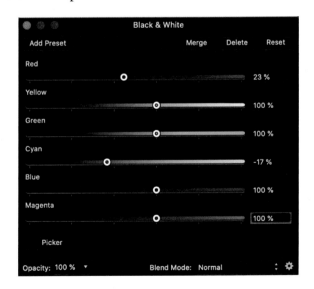

To see *before* & *after*:

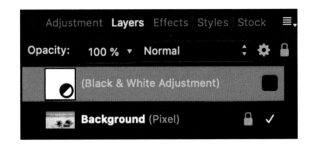

Go to the **Layers Panel** and *uncheck* & *check* the **top layer**. This image shows the top layer is deactivated, thus what you see on your screen is the full-color original image.

Remember: Active layers are always highlighted in blue, unless they're unchecked and thus invisible.

If you want to go back to an Adjustment layer because you'd like to tweak the values you changed:

Go back to the **Layers Panel** and simply *double-click* on the **preview thumbnail** (the white square on the top layer) for the Adjustment layer you want to go back to. Doing this action is simple because we only have two layers, but for edits that have multiple Adjustment layers, the action is the same.

When you do this, the pop-out window for that specific Adjustment will appear again.

Adjust the **sliders** however you want.

Close the Adjustment's **pop-out window** by *clicking* again on the **red button** in the top left corner of its pop-out window.

Another important thing to remember when using the Adjustments effectively is to know each Adjustment layer only affects the layers that are beneath it.

If you look at our Layers Panel, you'll see that the Black and White Adjustment layer is on top of our Background image of the seashells. This means our seashells look black and white because of where it's positioned in the Layers Panel.

Let's change their positions and see if there's any change to our image on the canvas.

To do this:

Click on the **Background layer** so it's highlighted in blue.

Drag it to the **top of the Layers Panel** (see the yellow arrow for this action). Notice how when you move this layer, it appears ethereal. This happens so you can see how and where to perfectly place your layer in the Layers Panel.

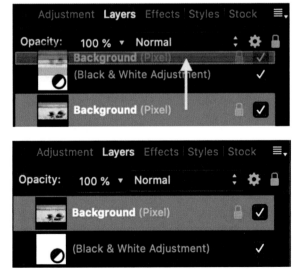

What effect does changing the positions in the Layers Panel have to do with how your image now looks?

Hopefully, you're seeing that your original Background image looks like it did before we worked with the Black and White Adjustment even though both layers are checked on.

The position is what matters, not whether the layers are checked on or not.

If you want the adjustment to affect your picture, you need to be sure the adjustment layer is above your picture.

To do this:

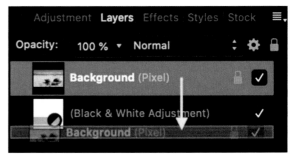

Click & *drag* the **bottom Background layer** below the Black & White Adjustment layer (see arrow for this action).

We're done using the **Black and White Adjustment** layer. So, we want to **delete** it. Here are three ways we can delete layers we no longer want:

1. *Highlight* the **layer** you want to delete and simply *press* **Delete** key on your keyboard.

2. *Highlight* a **layer** and *click* on the **Trashcan**.

3. *Highlight* a **layer** and *press* **Ctrl/Cmd+X.**

Hint: If you accidently delete a layer, simply *press* **Ctrl/Cmd+Z** to *undo* your last action.

Delete the **Black and White Adjustment layer** now if you haven't already.

We're going to now use a different Adjustment to continue this lesson.

Ready?

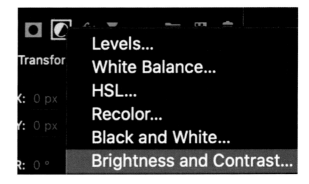

Go to the **icons bar** and *click* on the **Adjustments icon** again and *select* **Brightness and Contrast...**

To increase the **Brightness and Contrast**:

Adjust the **Brightness** slider to **25%.**

Adjust the **Contrast** slider to **41%.**

Press the **red button** to *close* the **window**.

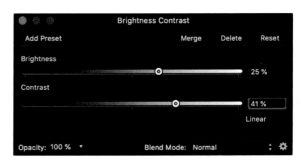

To see *before* & *after*:

    Go to the **Layers Panel**.

    Click the **Brightness/Contrast Adjustment** layer *off / on* (layer is unchecked).

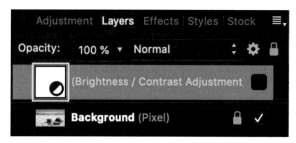

In this example, the **Brightness/Contrast** Adjustment is probably too strong.

To change this:

    Go to the **Layers Panel**.

    Double-click on the **preview thumbnail** on the Brightness/Contrast Adjustment's layer (see yellow square in above screenshot).

The pop-out window with the sliders will appear again.

    Move the **Brightness** to **13%**.

    Move the **Contrast** to **20%**.

    Press the **red button** to *close* the **window**.

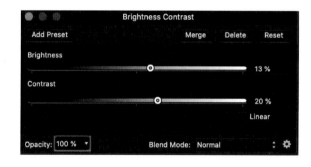

To see *before* & *after* (like we did at the top of this page):

    Go to the **Layers Panel**.

    Check the **Brightness/Contrast Adjustment** layer *off* & *on*.

As a final example of how the **Adjustments** layers work:

    Click on to **Adjustments icon** again.

    Select **HSL** to *change* the **saturation** of your picture.

    Move the **Saturation** slider to **28%**.

    Press the **red button** to *close* the **window**.

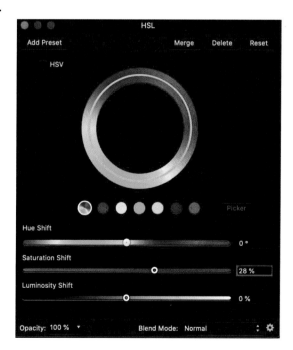

To see *before* & *after*.

Go to the **Layers Panel** & *click* the **HSL Shift Adjustment** layer *off* / *on*.

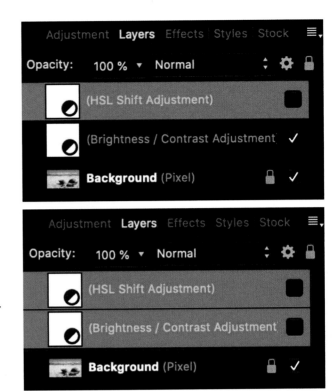

To see both the **HSL** and the **Brightness/Contrast Adjustment** layers *off* & *on* at the same time, *press* **Shift** and *select* **both of the adjustment layers**. Now, when you *click* on **one checked box**, both will respond jointly.

Done. This is our final image. You now know the basics of using adjustment layers.

Finished. This ends this tutorial.

Note: We will be using the same image of the seashells for the next tutorial. Please keep this image on your screen but go ahead and *delete* the **two Adjustment layers**.

Basics 6 – How to Use Masks

The 6th basic skill new users want to know is how to use Masks. When we first started working with this software, we had no idea what we were doing and a topic like masks made absolutely no sense to us at all.

Thankfully for you, we think we can easily explain and show you how to use masks, or so we hope :).

Before we get started, let's talk about masks and their functions:

What is the purpose of a mask?

Masks are used to **hide** or **reveal** parts of the layer.

Masks allow you to selectively *adjust* the **transparency** of a layer you are working with.

What are the two types of masks? **White & Black**.

What is the difference between the two? What are their functions?

White masks make the layer you are working on 100% **visible**.

Black masks make the layer you are working on 100% **invisible** or transparent.

Remember: **White** = visible   **Black** = invisible or transparent

That's the absolute basics of masks. Now, let's work with masks and see practically how they are applied to your work. We hope this tutorial will help you begin to understand how to use this powerful tool.

It's easier to show you than to explain how to use Masks with words.

Let's start:

Click on the **Background** layer so it's highlighted in blue (or active). It should already be so.

Go to the **icons bar** and *click* on the **mask icon** (it looks like a Japanese flag).

You should now see a **white** mask has been added to the Layers Panel and is now above the Background layer.

Note: If your Mask layer is not above the Background layer, but below-and-to-the-right, this is fixable. *Go* to the **right side of the Toolbar** and *click* on  the **Assistant** icon (see yellow rectangle). This will open a window with lots of menus. *Find* the **menu** named **"Adding mask layer to selection"** and *click* on the **option button** to its right and *select* **Add mask as new layer** - then *press* the **OK** button at the bottom right side of this pop-out window. Now, when you add a mask layer it will be placed above the active layer. Now you know where to go to order the layers (i.e., The Assistant).

Now, let's have some fun learning about masks:

Click on the **Paint Brush Tool** (or *press* **B**).

Set the **Foreground color** to **Black**. You can do this by either going to the Colors Studio where the Color Wheel is and *click* on the **black circle** that's interconnected and above a white circle (see yellow square).

You can also, if you set up two columns of Tools, *click* on the **black circle** located at the bottom of the Tools panel.

Note: If you wanted White to be the Foreground color, you'd simply *click* on the **White circle** and it'd replace itself above the black circle.

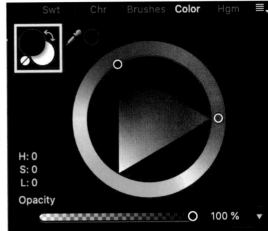

Hint: Try *pressing* the **X** key on your keyboard and watch what happens to the Black & White circles. Do you see how they change position? This is because the **X** key is the shortcut to swap Foreground & Background colors. Do not forget this shortcut. It is one of our favorites.

Now that we have our Foreground set to black, we can continue learning how to use Masks.

So, right now your Paint Brush Tool should be active and its color is black.

Paint (by *clicking* & *dragging*) **over the photograph**. This is what we did below. As you paint in black, on a white mask layer, where you paint you will make the area transparent. When you have layers beneath the mask layer, and you paint in black, you will remove the layer you are painting on to reveal the layer beneath your current layer.

Let's change the Foreground to White by *pressing* the **X** key to show you the opposite effect.

   Paint in **white** over the areas of the image we painted in black. As you do this, you will see that the seashells image will come back to its original image.

Now, our image has returned back to its original form:

Now that we've working on adding a mask to an image layer, let's now add a mask to an Adjustment layer. We'll start this on the next page.

But first we need to delete this mask layer. Do you remember the three ways to delete layers?

1. *Highlight* the **layer** you want to delete and simply *press* **Delete** key on your keyboard.

2. *Highlight* a **layer** and *click* on the **Trashcan.**

3. *Highlight* a **layer** and *press* **Ctrl/Cmd+X.**

Ok. Now our Layers Panel should only have the Background image of the shells in it.

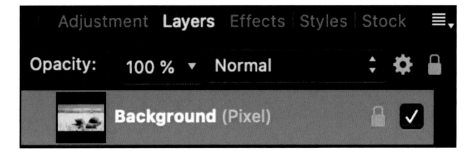

This is how you add a mask to an Adjustments layer.

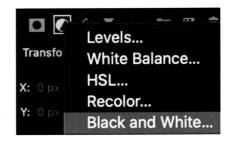

Go to the **icons bar** and *click* on the **Adjustments icon** and then *select* **Black and White**...

Press the **red button** to *close* the **pop-out window** that will appear. We won't be making any refinements. We chose this Adjustment just to make our image black & white.

Note: It's important to know that every Adjustment layer in Affinity Photo comes with a pre-built mask (look at how there is a white preview thumbnail on the Adjustment layer's left side - this represents a white mask). What this means is that we can immediately paint in black or white to hide or show its adjustment properties. This is probably a confusing concept, so we'll explain as we go.

We are about to start again. Make sure the Paint Brush Tool is selected and the **Foreground** color is set to **black**. Use the shortcut of X to switch between the Fore-/Background circles.

Paint over **the shell in the lower right-hand corner** of the four shells. As you paint in black, you will be removing the Black & White Adjustment from the layer to reveal the color of the shell underneath.

Here is what we did when we painted over this shell. As you can see, painting in black reveals the color image below the top Adjustment layer.

Oops, we accidently painted on part of the shell above the bottom-right shell. Do you know what we can do to fix this?

Answer: If you thought to change the Foreground color to white and paint over the parts of the upper shell we painted in black on, you'd be correct.

Press the **X key** to *change* the **Foreground** color to **White**.

Paint in **white** over the area on the top shell to hide the color layer beneath and fix the mistake we made.

Review: Paint Brush Adjustments (Width, Opacity, Flow, Hardness)

<u>Width</u> is the size of the Brush's circular cursor. *Use* the **bracket keys** to make smaller or larger.

<u>Opacity</u> is the see-throughness of the color (or layer).

<u>Flow</u> is how much paint comes out of the brush each time you *click* & *drag* the **brush** over the image.

<u>Hardness</u> relates to the sides of the brush stroke. 100% has fine edges. 0% has fuzzy edges.

To delete the current shell image, press **Ctrl/Cmd+W** and *click* on **Don't Save** button.

Finished. This ends this tutorial. Masks are very confusing for beginners. Trust us, it will get easier.

Basics 7 - How to Make Selections

Making selections is one of the most-used skills you'll need to know how to do. We love working with the **Selection Brush Tool** in Affinity Photo. It's so easy to use and so powerful. This is the Tool you'll use the most when making one portion of your document stand out or be cut out and placed in another scene. This is why we've added this tutorial to the basics. Here are the names of the images we'll be using for this lesson. **Basics 7 - Moon & Basic 7 - Ship**. Please have the moon image uploaded to your screen so we can start. Here are the current hyperlinks to these images:

https://pixabay.com/photos/moon-sky-night-moonlight-nature-2913221/

https://pixabay.com/photos/purple-ship-sailing-ship-3054804/

Ready to begin...

Press **Ctrl/Cmd+J** to *duplicate* our original **Background image**.

Select the **Selection Brush Tool**.

Go to the **Contextual Toolbar** and look for **Mod**e: Make sure **Add** is *clicked on*.

Note: We use these two buttons (**Add & Subtract**) when we want to make more precise selections and have maybe selected too much or not enough. We will use these two buttons further on. The yellow rectangle is around the Add icon.

Go to the **Contextual Toolbar** and *click* on **Width** to *increase* your brush's width to half the size of the moon. While you are on the Contextual Toolbar, look to the right of and...

Click on the **Snap to edges** icon (see yellow rectangle) also found on the Contextual Toolbar. This will make the dancing ants fit the outline of any object you want to select. This is a very important device for all selections.

Click & *drag* the **Selection Brush Tool** in a small circle inside the moon. This will create a selection of the moon's borders.

The selection that was made of the moon is very good. Sure, there may be some parts of it that could be better, but for this introductory lesson, we'll use what the software has given us. Later on in this book we'll work with refining selections, and you'll get more practice with this skill. Now, we're going to duplicate our selected moon layer and in doing so the selection will be duplicated but not the background. This is a quick and easy way of removing the background from an image.

Press **Ctrl/Cmd+J** to *duplicate* the **Moon layer**.

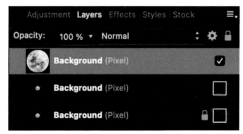

Uncheck the **two lower layers** (see two yellow squares) to *remove* the **background** and leave us with only the selected moon with its dancing ants on a transparent background.

Press **Ctrl/Cmd+D** to *deselect* the **dancing ants**.

This ends this first part of How to Make Selections. We'll continue working with our currently selected moon image in the next tutorial. Yes, making basic selections like this is how it's done. More complex selections with hair, fur, or trees are another much more involved type of selection process we'll show you later.

Basics 8 – How to Change the Background of a Photo

Whenever you make a selection around an object, that selection gives you many possibilities, like, to change its color, cut it out of its current photo, add it to a new photo, and to make many different adjustments and edits to it that are unique to only the selected item.

In this next lesson, we'll show you how to take this selected moon and add it to another image. The process of selecting an object(s), persons, or things is the same as we just did above.

Because our moon is now surrounded by a transparent layer, we can now copy this image and place it on top of any other image. The new image will essentially fill the transparent area around the moon giving the appearance that the moon fits to that new image.

Click on the **Move Tool** and make it active (shortcut is V).

Press **Ctrl/Cmd+C** anywhere on our moon image to *copy* it.

Open the **purple sailboat** image.

Press **Ctrl/Cmd+V** to *paste* our **moon image** onto the sailboat image.

When we do this, our moon will be three things: Too large; in the wrong position; and not the right color to match the scene.

To fix these three issues:

Click on the **Move tool** (or *use* its shortcut **V**) so we can move the moon image.

Move the **moon** image to the top-right corner of the image (see yellow arrow for direction).

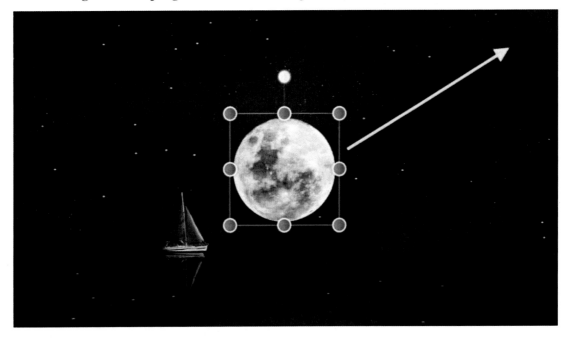

Click on one of the **corner blue nodes** and shrink the moon to a little smaller size than the sailboat.

The moon is looking very good, but we can make it match the scene even better by changing its Opacity so its white color isn't so stark and so it blends into the scene much better.

Click on the **top layer** so it's highlighted in blue.

Change its **Opacity** to **50**%. Now, our moon is starting to fit into the image.

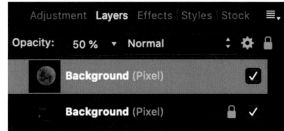

There's just one more thing to do and that's to make it have its own reflecting shadow on the surface of the water. The sailboat has one and so the moon should have one, too. Because the moon layer is already highlighted in blue, this is what we'll do.

Press **Crtl/Cmd+J** to *duplicate* the **moon's layer**.

Select the **Move Tool** (or *press* **V**) and *click* on the **moon image** & *drag* it **below the surface of the water**.

Change its **Opacity** to **10**% to make it look faded in the water. How easy was that.

Let's review what we just did.

1. We used the Selection Brush Tool to make a simple selection of our moon.

2. We duplicated its image so the only the moon remained. Then we deselected the dancing ants.

3. We copied this selection and pasted it on another image, where we changed its Opacity to blend in with the colors of the sailboat image. Then we duplicated this moon and make it look like a reflection in the water.

Done. This is our final image.

Note: When you're done with this lesson, go ahead and delete this image from your screen. We are done with it.

Finished. This ends this tutorial.

Bonus Lesson: How to Make Selections Using the Pen Tool

Here is the webpage to the image we'll be using for this tutorial

https://pixabay.com/photos/present-package-gift-celebration-1893640/

Ok. You should have the image of the two presents on your Affinity Photo screen.

Note: Before we start, we want you to know that using the **Pen Tool** for doing selections should only be done to objects that have definite edges. We use this technique when the background and the object we are selecting blend into each other making using the **Selection Brush Tool** difficult. This image of the present is not one such image we are talking about, but we will use this image because it is a good teaching image to learn how to use the Pen Tool.

Ready? Let's start...

Select the **Pen Tool** (or *press* **P**).

Go to the **Contextual Toolbar** & *click* on the **Pen Mode** button (see yellow rectangle).

Click & *draw* your **outline** around the red present, only. Not both.

When you get back around to where you started, make sure you *click* on the **first node** that you started with.

Hint: Try to draw within the red present's perimeter by a pixel and not on the outside of its perimeter (see image below for what we mean). You don't want the background to be a part of the soon-to-be cut-out object.

This may be your first time using this tool, so give yourself a break and don't worry at all if you're able to do a perfect job or not. The Pen Tool is the most precise selection tool and it'll take a few months or years of practice to be an expert at. Just take your time and do as good of a job as you can.

Note: When you're done, make sure you *press* **ESC** on your keyboard. This tells Affinity Photo that the selection process is over and that when you *click* on the **canvas** again, a new selection path will start. We can't stress enough that you make sure you've *clicked* on the **first node** to finish your selection before you *press* **ESC**. This is a learning process, but a frustrating one if you don't do it right.

Let's suppose your job at doing the outline of the perimeter wasn't as perfect as you'd like it to be. Let us show you what you can do to go back and fix any errors.

First, *zoom in* to your **object** by *pressing* **Ctrl/Cmd +** (see the yellow rectangle).

Select the **Node Tool**.

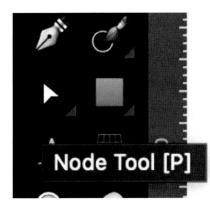

When using the **Node Tool**, hover it on the line between two nodes and a perpendicular small line will appear (see left image below). It is this exact spot on the line that you can bend the line to however you want it (see right image). It takes practice, but we hope you understand.

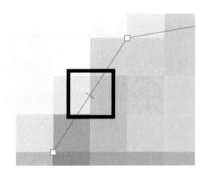

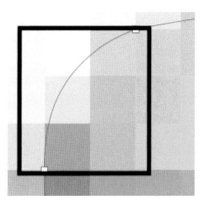

Hint: While practice does makes perfect, when we are making selections with curves while using the **Pen Tool**, we won't worry too much about exact precision. We make the two nodes at the start and the end of the curve and when the whole selection has been made, then we go back and change the curves to our standards.

Let's get back to the tutorial: When you're done changing the nodes into the curves you are satisfied with...

Go to the **Contextual Toolbar** & *click* on **Selection**. This will create a line of dancing ants where you made your selection.

Go to the **Toolbar** and *click* on the **Assistant icon** and *change* the **position** of a Mask Layer to **Add mask as a child layer**.

Go to the **icons bar** and *click* on the **mask icon**. This will cause the background to be immediately removed. Notice how different the Mask layer looks like in the Layers Panel.

Press **Ctrl/Cmd+D** to *deselect* the **dancing ants**.

To change the background to a different color of your choosing...

Click on **Add Pixel Layer** (next to the **Trashcan**).

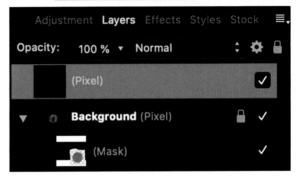

This is what our Layers Panel should look like now:

Go to the **Menu bar** - **Edit** - **Fill...** A pop-out window will appear that looks like this.

Click on the **white color rectangle** to *change* the **color of the fill**. When you *click* on this **rectangle**, the Color Wheel pop-out window will open.

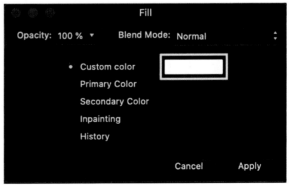

Move the **Hue node** to a deep blue color. The Hue node is the node on outside circle. The node in the inner triangle adjusts the saturation & luminosity of whatever Hue you choose.

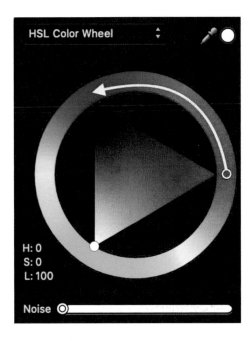

Click **Apply** to set the color you want as the fill.

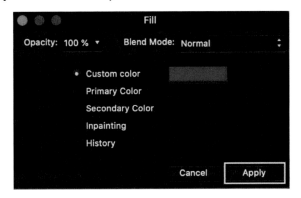

Last step.

Go to the **Layers Panel** and *click* on **top Pixel layer** & *drag* it to the **bottom** of the Layers Stack. This is what our Layers Panel looks like now:

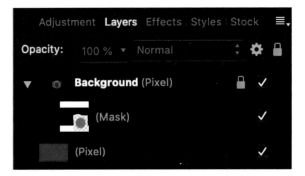

Done. This is our final image.

Note: Please either save this image or delete it using the shortcut of Ctrl/Cmd+W. We won't use it again.

Finished. This ends this bonus tutorial.

Basics 9 – How to Add Text to an Image

Adding text to an image is one of the most basic, but most used skills photo editors use from all things personal and commercial. Thankfully, Affinity Photo makes this a very simple process. Please upload the image for this lesson onto your screen. The name is **Basics 9 - Woman**. Here is the current hyperlink:

https://cdn.pixabay.com/photo/2014/12/16/22/25/woman-570883_1280.jpg

In this tutorial, we are going to add the text "Each day is a new beginning" to our image.

To add this text:

Select the **Artistic Text Tool** (or *press* **T**).

Click & *drag* on the **picture** to specify how big the text you want to be. Notice how the first letter is created by a *click* & *drag* **motion**. If you don't get the right font size on the first go, it's no problem because Affinity Photo makes resizing text super easy. You can see that our current font size is **188.5 pt** by looking at the text bubble next to our **A**.

Type our **phrase** "Each day is a new beginning." without the quotation marks. As you can see, our phrase has gone way out to the right-side of our image. All we need to do is to *click* on one of the **right-side top or bottom blue nodes** & *drag* our **phrase** back into within the borders of our image.

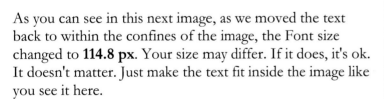

As you can see in this next image, as we moved the text back to within the confines of the image, the Font size changed to **114.8 px**. Your size may differ. If it does, it's ok. It doesn't matter. Just make the text fit inside the image like you see it here.

If you want to change the color of the text, simply *click* on the **Text layer** so it's highlighted in blue (already is) and then *move* the **Color Wheel** to the color of your choice. We'll choose a pink.

Now we'll walk you through how to do this.

Click on the **top layer** so it's highlighted in blue (assuming it isn't already).

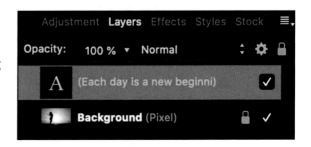

40

Oops, we misspelt Beginning. To fix this, simply *click* on the **text** make your correction by adding a "ng".

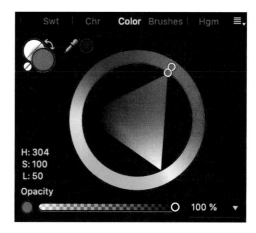

Go to the **Color Wheel** & *move* the **outside hue node** to **pink**.

That's it! Adding text to an image is really this simple. Affinity Photo makes this process easy. We'll get more practice with adding text later in this book.

Done. This is our final image. You now know how to add text to an image. Affinity makes this process quite simple. What do you think?

Note: We will be using this final image in our last basic skill. Please save it as an **.afphoto** file or keep it on your screen for the next lesson or just turn the page and we'll continue with the basics.

To do that, *go* to the **Menu bar - File - Save As...** and *choose* **where** you want to save the image and *press* **Save**.

Finished. This ends this tutorial.

Basics 10 – How to Save & Export

The 10th skill beginners need to know is <u>how to save & export.</u>

For this tutorial, we are going to use the final image from the previous tutorial. Please have it uploaded to your canvas now if it isn't already. Now, we're going to show you how to save & export this image in the various file formats. Affinity Photo makes this a very simple process.

To save the image so you can come back and work on it later in Affinity Photo:

Go to **File**.

Select **Save As** from the drop-down menu. This will save your photo as an **Affinity Photo** file where you can continue working later (see the white rectangle).

Note: These Affinity Photo files are much larger than .jpeg or .png files but are necessarily larger because they contain all of different layers and effects you've made to your image.

When you are completely done with your image and want to **export** it in a different file format:

Go to **Menu bar** - **File Menu bar** - **Export** (see yellow rectangle in above image).

Before we continue in this tutorial, it's important for you to understand the different file formats you can save your image as.

Affinity Photo has a range of formats that you can use to export.

The two most common formats are **PNG** and **JPEG**.

JPEG is useful because it converts your picture into a small size file (i.e., the images typically found in books). Their characteristics are: Smaller file sizes, fast loading times, no transparency retained, compressed image.

PNG is useful because preserves transparency (in plain English: there will be a white & grey checkered background to an object). Their characteristics are: Larger file sizes because they contain more information, retain transparent parts of an image, overall better and higher quality images.

The key difference is this. Most of the time we use JPEGs but in rare cases when we want to keep a transparent part of the image transparent when we save it and later reopen it, we use PNG.

This is what the **Export** window looks like. Here you can see all the different file types you can export your image as. Go ahead and *click* on **any file format** you want and you'll see the export options change. Don't worry if the File Size numbers are different on your screen.

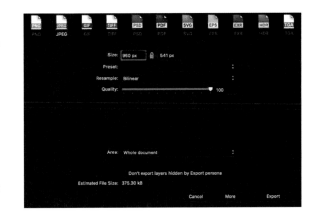

Hint: We recommend you frequent the official Affinity Help website for other search for the meaning of each of these types of files (and any other question you have about Affinity Photo).

https://affinity.help/photo/en-US.lproj/index.html

As a rule of thumb, for us at KuhlmanPublishing, we normally use the .png when we want to keep an image's transparent background and .jpeg when we want the whole image (as opposed to just a selected item in a photo).

Getting back to the image we want to **export**, let's:

Export this **picture** of the water as a **.jpeg** since we will be exporting the whole image and we don't care about transparency.

Since we've selected **JPEG** from the top line of file format choices, the most important part now is the size of our image. Our image is only **375.30 kB** (see bottom left of above image), so it's pretty small.

But many images you'll work with are huge (**<25 mb**) and in order for you to email them using Affinity Photo, you'll need to first lower their size.

To do this:

Click on the **Preset** window (see partially hidden yellow rectangle). A drop-down menu will appear.

Choose **JPEG (High Quality)**. Immediately, you'll see that the file size has dropped dramatically.

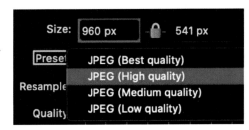

The image size is probably cut down by half or more. Now we have very small file to export.

Click on the **Export** button in the lower right-hand corner of the Export pop-out window.

Type a **name** of your picture in the **Save As** field (ours is "Image with text.").

Choose **Where** to *store* your **file**.

Press **Save** to *export* the **file** to your computer.

Note: Depending on which type of operating system, your **Save As** and **Export** windows will look a bit different, but the effect is the same.

Special Tutorial: How to Create Specialized Shortcuts (if you don't have a US keyboard).

We created this special tutorial because we, too, want shortcuts to increase the Width of our brushes like how the majority of our readers can use the bracket keys. This lesson can be applied to any shortcut key stroke you'd rather have than the ones assigned to you.

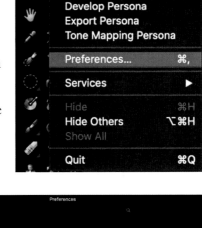

We live in Germany, so our keyboard layout doesn't have any bracket keys. Where these keys are, you can find the German Ö and the Ä. Very different-looking letters from our native English language.

Let's get started.

Click on the **Affinity Photo tab** at the far top left of the   screen & *click* on **Preferences.**

After opening **Preferences**, there will be another drop-down window where you'll need to *choose* a box labelled **Keyboard Shortcuts.**

Click on **Keyboard Shortcuts** and then you'll need to *click* on the **second drop-down menu** in the top left of the new screen (see yellow rectangle in image below).

Choose the **Paint Brush Tool** (highlighted in blue).

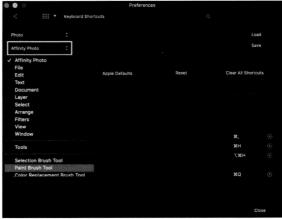

Here you'll have to find buttons on the keyboard that are not being used.

What did we do? We used the German letters **Ö** & **Ä** for our two shortcuts. Yes, we are native English speakers, but we live & work in Germany. German QWERTZ keyboards don't have bracket keys.

Note: This change of the shortcut letters is the same for all languages and keyboards. Follow these steps and make the changes as you see fit.

Finished. This ends this tutorial & the first section of this book.

Tutorial 1: How to Create a Double Exposure Effect

In this tutorial, we're going to learn how to apply a double exposure effect. This is the cover image for our best-selling book, The Affinity Photo Manual. What you learn here is exactly how we made our cover image.

Please upload the two images we'll be using for this lesson named **Tutorial 1 - Eagle** & **Tutorial 1 -Mountains**. Here are the hyperlinks to their images:

https://pixabay.com/photos/bald-eagle-raptor-head-close-up-2715461/

https://pixabay.com/photos/zugspitze-alpine-summit-1048995/

Ready?

Ok, let's begin by opening both images onto Affinity Photo. We will be working with the image of the eagle first. Each image will have its own tab at the top of the canvas.

We want the eagle's image to go from left to right and not the way it is.

To change this:

Go to the **Menu bar - Document - Flip Horizontal**. Yes, we edited this screenshot. The option is all the way at the bottom of the list.

First, we need to remove the background.

To do this:

Select the **Selection Brush Tool** and set the **Mode** to **Add** (see yellow rectangle).

Paint over the **eagle** adjusting the width of the brush so you can get to the tip of its beak.

Go to the **Contextual Toolbar** and click on **Refine...**

Brush over the **edges** of the eagle so all feathers and beak are more clearly selected.

This is what our eagle looks like after we used the Refine Selection Brush. The edges should be crisp and clean.

If your subject is red, then you need to press **Cancel** and invert your **pixel selection** by pressing **Ctrl/Cmd+Shift+I**. Then, when you press **Refine**, your subject will be in color and the background in red.

Press **Apply** in the bottom-right corner of the Refine Selection pop-out window when done.

Now, look at the Layers Panel and make sure the single layer is selected and highlighted in blue.

Go to the **Toolbar** and *click* on the **Assistant**.

Change the **position** of the mask layer so it's a child layer and not a new layer that stacks at the top of the Layers Panel (see yellow rectangle for the correct button).

Press **Close** to set the change.

Go to the **icons bar** and *click* on the **mask icon**.

Deselect your **selection** by *pressing* **Ctrl/Cmd+D**.

This is what our image looks like now.

Click on the **top layer** so it's highlighted in blue. The mask layer will also be highlighted.

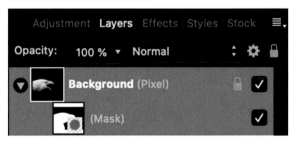

Duplicate this **top layer** by *pressing* **Ctrl/Cmd+J**.

Click on the **Mountains tab** so the image is right in front of you.

Move your **cursor** anywhere on the canvas & *press* **Crtl/Cmd+C** to *copy* this **image**.

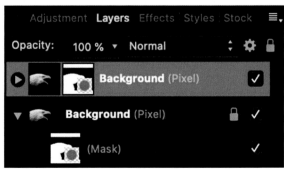

Go back to our **eagle image** & *press* **Ctrl/Cmd+V** to *paste* the **mountains image** on top of our eagle image.

Go to the **Layers Panel** and *click* & *drag* the **Mountain background layer** underneath-and-to-the-right of the very bottom Mask layer. Make sure it is not directly underneath the Mask layer. We want it under the Mask layer and-to-the-right. This special movement of layers creates a child layer. Child layers are layers that only affect the layer it is attached to, its Parent Layer, and not the other layers in the Layers Panel (see yellow arrow for this motion).

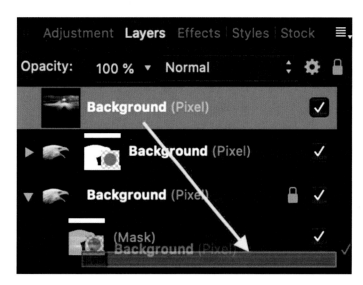

Uncheck the **top layer** and *select* the **Move Tool** (or *press* **V**) to *move* the **Mountain image** around however you want it to be placed underneath your subject. We've added a shot of the Layers Panel so you can see that the top layer is unchecked.

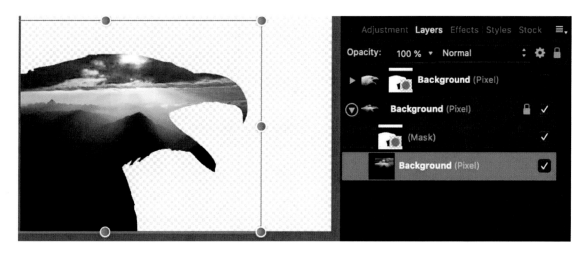

When you're done moving your Mountain image to where you want it, *check* the **top layer** back on and highlight it in blue as well by clicking on it. This is a very important step!

Did you remember to do the last step? We hope you did.

Change the **Blend Mode** to **Average** by *clicking* on **the area we placed the yellow rectangle over** and *select* **Average** from the drop-down menu. It's near the bottom of the list. This will blend our eagle image with our mountain image to create the effect we are after.

 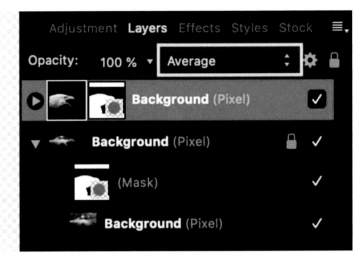

Go to the **icons bar** and *click* on the **Adjustments icon** and *select* **Levels**. It's the first in the list.

Adjust the **Black Level** to around **15%**.

Adjust the **White Level** to around **85%**.

Click on the **red button** to *close* this **window**.

These adjustments will increase the detail and the contrast.

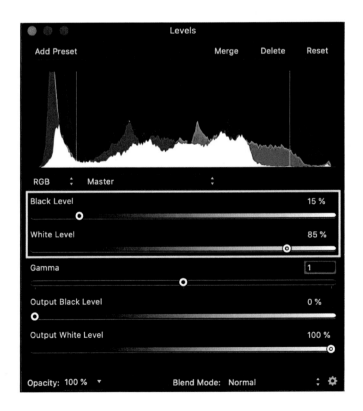

The last step we're going to take is to create a nice black background with a red/black gradient.

Note: Pay attention to how we do this next step. This technique of changing a background's color is one we do very often in Affinity Photo. Once you learn it, it's actually very simple.

Ready to change the background?

Click on the **Rectangle Tool** (or *press* **U**) and *click* & *drag* a **rectangle** over our whole image.

This is what our image looks like now after doing this step:

Go the **Colors Studio** & *move* the **inner color node** straight up vertically so the color of the rectangle changes to black (see white arrow for this action).

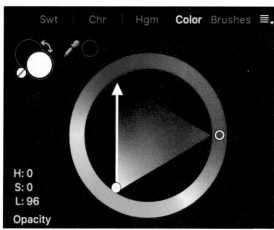

Note: Maybe your Color Wheel doesn't look exactly like ours. That's ok. Just move the inner node into the black area of the inner triangle.

This is what our Layers Panel looks like now. Notice how the preview thumbnail for the Rectangle layer shows the Rectangle is all black. This is what we want.

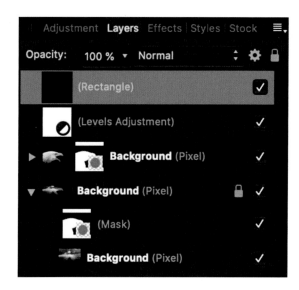

We're almost done, just a few more steps.

Click & *drag* the **top Rectangle layer** to the bottom of the Layers Stack. Make sure the left-side of the Rectangle layer is all the way to the left. We want this to be its own independent layer and not a Child.

Click on the **bottom Rectangle layer** so it's highlighted in blue.

Select the **Gradient Tool** from the Tools.

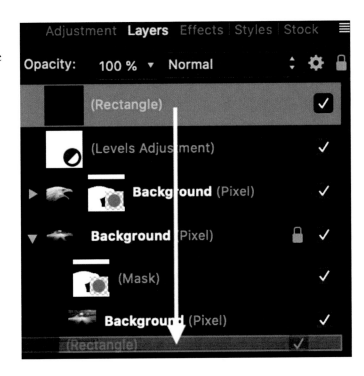

Click once on the **right-side border** of our image & *drag* the **gradient line** across the center of our image stopping on the left-side border. If you *hold down* the **Shift key** when drawing this gradient line, the line will be perfectly flat. Maybe both of your circular nodes are black and not gray/black as you see here.

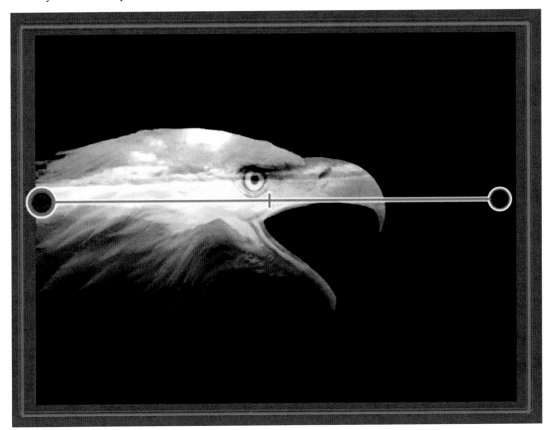

Click on the **left gradient node** that's on the left border and on the eagle's neck so it's bigger than the right node. When you see one gradient node that's bigger than the other(s), then you know that gradient node is selected.

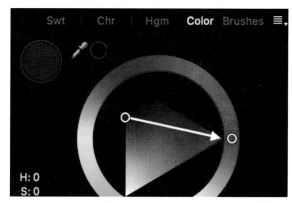

Go to the **Colors Studio** & *move* the **inner color node** to the position nearest the Hue node (see our white arrow for this action). This will cause the selected gradient node to change its color from gray to red.

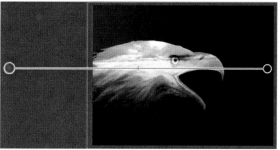

The red a bit too bright, so let's move the red gradient node further out into the canvas away from our image to decrease the brightness. See how the left node is no longer inside the borders of the photo, but extending to the left in the canvas area? This is what we mean.

Done.

This is what our final Layers Panel looks like.

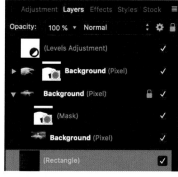

This is our final image. How do you like the look?

Final Adjustment:

If you want to reposition the mountain image inside the Eagle, *click* on the **Move Tool** and then *click* on the **Background layer** directly above the bottom Rectangle layer and then use a *click* & *drag* action to **reposition the mountain image** where you want it.

Note: We are done with this image. Save it. Export it. Delete it. Do whatever you want. We don't need it for the next lesson.

Finished. This ends this tutorial.

Tutorial 2: How to Create a Color Splash Effect

Have you ever seen photographs where one object is in color while the rest of the content is black and white? If so, that effect is a powerful one and a simple one. In this lesson, we're going to show you the best way to create this effect and when you're done, we hope you can sit back and say to yourself: "I think I'm beginning to see the power of masks." The name of the image for this lesson is **Tutorial 2 - Car**. Please have it uploaded to your screen now. Here is the webpage to the image we'll be using:

https://pixabay.com/photos/car-racing-motorsport-racing-car-4394450/

Ok. Ready? Please have this image uploaded and on your screen. Here are the steps to do this very cool technique:

Choose the **object** you want to select. In this image it'll be the front car.

Select the **Pen Tool**.

Click the **outline** of the car. Review **Basics #7** if you need the help.

Take your time and practice using the Pen Tool. Remember that you can use the Node Tool to add curvatures between the white anchor point nodes.

Go to the **Contextual Toolbar** and *click* on **Selection** (see yellow rectangle).

Go to the **Menu bar - Select - Invert Pixel Selection**.

Note: *Inverting* the pixel selection will choose everything in the photo except the car you just selected.

Go to the **icons bar** and *click* on the **Adjustments icon** & *select* **Black and White...**

Click on the **red button** to *close* the **pop-out window**. We won't be making any refining adjustments; we only wanted to make our image black & white.

Go to the **Menu bar - Select - Deselect** (the dancing ants will disappear).

52

Done. This is our final image. Impressive, isn't it?

Want to try this technique another way without screenshots?

Delete the **final image** and *reload* **it** on your screen.

Press **Ctrl/Cmd+J** to *duplicate* the **image's layer**.

Go to the **icons bar** and *click* on the **Adjustments icon** and *select* **Black and White...**

Close the **Black and White** pop-out window.

Click on the **Paint Brush Tool** and *set* the **Foreground** color to **black**.

Paint on the **car** we want to colorize. That's it. If you go over the car, *change* the **Foreground** color to **white** and paint to correct any errors.

Done.

Which is the better technique? We prefer the first because it's a lot more precise. But the second can be done in about 20 seconds once you've done it more than once.

Note: We are done with this image. Please save it or delete it so we can start afresh in the next lesson.

Finished. This ends this tutorial.

Tutorial 3: How to Create a Stylish Duotone Effect

In this tutorial we'll going to learn how to create a stylish duotone effect. It's a cool effect and we hope you like it, too. Please have the image named **Tutorial 3 - Guitar** uploaded to your screen so we can begin. Here is the webpage for this tutorial: **https://pixabay.com/photos/guitar-classical-guitar-756326/**

Once you have this image uploaded onto your canvas, we'll begin.

Go to the **icons bar** and *click* on the **Adjustments icon** & *select* **Black and White**...

We aren't going to be making any adjustments from the pop-out window with the sliders. Just *press* on the **red X** in the pop-out window to get rid of this window. The image is now **Black & White**, which is what we want.

Click again on the **Adjustments icon** and in the drop-down menu *select* **Gradient Map**. This will cause our image to look very strange (see this image here).

When you choose **Gradient Map**, its own pop-out window will appear. When you look at this window, there in the top is a color bar with **red** on the left side, **green** in the middle and **blue** on the right side.

Here is what each color stands for:

   Red: Shadows   **Green**: Mid-tones   **Blue**: Highlights

For this tutorial, since it's a duotone effect (**duo** meaning **two**), we need to delete one of these Gradient Map nodes. The likely candidate is the middle node.

   Click on the **middle green node** (see black square) & *click* on the **Delete button** located in the Gradient Map pop-out window (see yellow rectangle).

Note: Do not press the Delete key on your keyboard.

Then *press* on the **Reverse** button located below the Delete button. This will cause the respective colors (red & blue) to reflect different aspects. Reds will now represent the highlights & Blue will represent the shadows.

This is what our image should look like now:

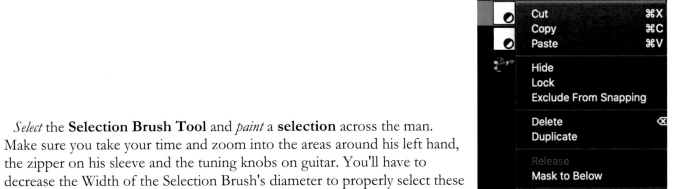

We now have a beautiful duotone effect, but let's see if we can make it even better. To do this, we're going to **Merge** all layers into one visible layer.

Here's how:

Right-click on **any layer** and *select* **Merge Visible**.

Select the **Selection Brush Tool** and *paint* a **selection** across the man. Make sure you take your time and zoom into the areas around his left hand, the zipper on his sleeve and the tuning knobs on guitar. You'll have to decrease the Width of the Selection Brush's diameter to properly select these minute details.

Take your time and try to do your best.

Pro Tip: *Hold-down* the **Option/Alt** key to do the opposite action so when you *click* to **paint the selection**, you'll remove parts of the selection instead of adding.

Note: Knowing how to refine selections takes a very long time to master. So, take your time and do as best you can. Over time, you'll get better and better. We are still learning, too. For this lesson, don't worry if your selection isn't perfect.

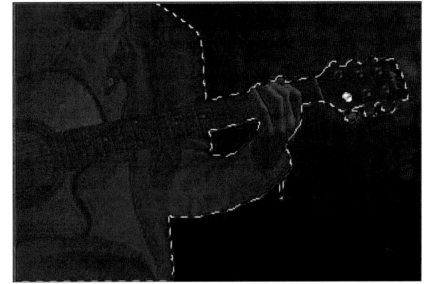

Go to the **Contextual Toolbar** & *click* on **Refine...** This will allow us to make our selection more precise. But, for this tutorial, total precision isn't necessary since we're only working with two colors.

Paint over the **technical parts** (fingers, zipper, tuning knobs) & then *click* on **Apply**. When you're done, hopefully these more difficult parts will be better selected. One caveat you need to know is that when trying to refine selections where the foreground & background colors are hard to distinguish, the Refine Selection Brush Tool isn't the end all, end all.

This is our selection. Try your best to make yours like ours.

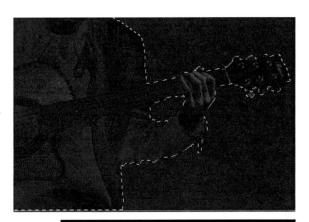

Note: You may need, as in this case, go back and again use the Selection Brush Tool and paint in the selection around the areas the Refine Selection Tool missed or improperly marked. Thankfully, for most of the time the Refine Selection Tool works wonders.

Make sure the (Pixel) layer is at the top of our Layers Panel before continuing.

Go to the **icons bar** and *click* on the **mask icon.**

Press **Ctrl/Cmd+D** to *deselect* the **dancing ants**.

This is what our Layers Panel should look like now:

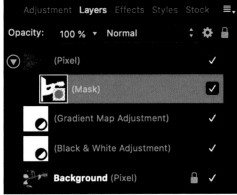

It doesn't look like much has happened but if we *select* the **bottom three layers** and then *turn them off* you can see that we have just the man with the guitar on the top Layer with a transparent background.

Click these **layers** back on and let's get rid of the dancing ants by *pressing* **Deselect (Ctrl/Cmd+D).**

You can also *deselect* by going to the **Menu bar** -**Select** -**Deselect.**

For this next creative part, make sure the bottom three layers are *selected* in **blue** (see image to the right). If you forgot how to do this, *click* on the **bottom layer** so it's highlighted, then while *holding-down* the **Shift key** *click* on the **Gradient Map layer.**

Click on the **small triangle** on the Rectangle Tool's icon (see small yellow square) and a drop-down menu will appear.

Select the **Ellipse Tool** (looks like a circle).

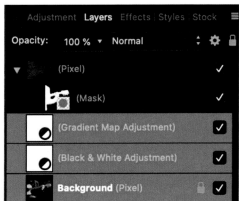

What we are going to do now is add some shapes to the image to make it more interesting. In this case, round balls. To make this work, all three bottom layers need to be active.

Click & *drag* a **circle** about the size of the man's extended hand. This ball will appear behind the man's arm. Look at our image to see what we want you to do.

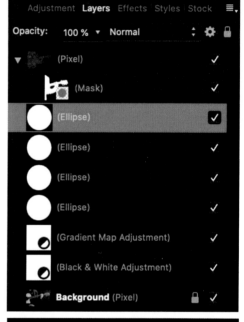

Press **Ctrl/Cmd+J** <u>three times</u> to create four of these balls. After you do this there should be four Ellipse layers.

Hint: Remember. If you want to *create* perfectly symmetrical shapes, *hold down* the **Shift** button when you *drag* out your **shapes**.

This is what our Layers Panel looks like now.

Select all **Ellipse layers** so they're all highlighted in blue. Use the Shift key method we just taught you how to use.

Press the **3** key on your keyboard. This shortcut will immediately change the Opacity of all selected layers to 30%.

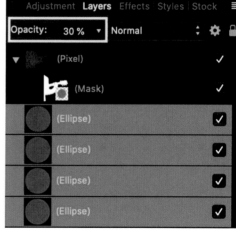

Hint: There are three ways to adjust Opacity:

1. *Press* the **3** key on the keyboard.

2. *Click* on the **downward-pointing triangle** (inside the yellow rectangle) to the right of the 30% and use the pop-out slider to move the Opacity to the level you want.

3. *Triple-click* **inside the value box** (also within the yellow rectangle) where it now has 30%. This will cause the number to be highlighted in blue. Then you can type the % you want.

Click the **cursor** <u>anywhere inside the canvas area</u> to *deactivate* the **four Ellipse layers**.

We're now going to add color to each Ellipse layer and reposition them on the right side of the image. We'll tell you how to colorize one and then you add any color you want to the other three.

Click on the **top Ellipse layer** so it's active and then *go* to the **Color Wheel** and *click* on the **outside ring** where **red** is. This action will cause the circle (or Ellipse) turn red.

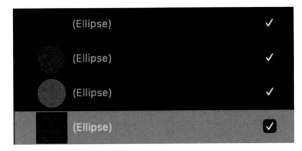

Click & *drag* this **circle** <u>down by the guitarist's leg</u>.

Now it's your turn to do these steps for the other three circles. This is what our four Ellipse layers look like after we colored each of ours. We chose red, pink, yellow, and a dark blue. We shrank three and kept one the same size. Remember to hold-down the Shift key when resizing the circles to keep their original aspect ratios.

The last thing we want to do is darken the **Background**.

Click on the **bottom Background layer** so it's highlighted in blue.

Go to the **icons bar** and *click* on the **Adjustments icon** & *choose* **Brightness and Contrast...** When its pop-out window appears...

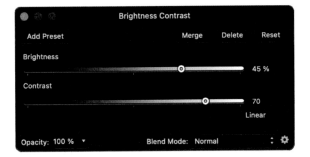

Increase the **Brightness** to **45%**

Increase the **Contrast** to **70%**.

Note: Play around with the two sliders. Maybe you'd like to have a different look than ours. That's totally ok.

Done. This is our final image.

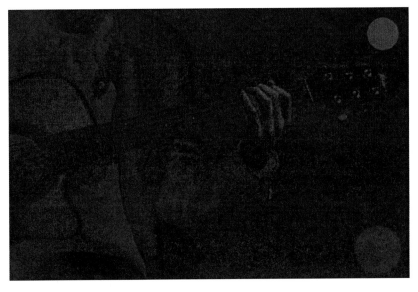

Finished. This ends this tutorial.

Tutorial 4: How to Create a Matte Image Effect

Every time you go process your photographs, you're given the choice of Glossy or Matte.

The difference everybody knows is that one is shinny and the other, well, not. But there is an actual difference in the photo processing. Matte images are designed to minimize the reflection of light and it does this by a special coating placed on top of a photograph when processed from digital to print.

Glossy photographs are the polar opposite: They are specifically designed to reflect as much light as possible.

In this lesson, we'll show you how to make any photograph have a Matte look. We've included in this lesson how the matte photograph will look like in black and white, too. We'll also explore the difference between using a simply Black and White adjustment layer with & without tweaking of the different hues in the photo.

Please have the image named **Tutorial 4 - Woman** uploaded to your screen so we can begin. Here is the current hyperlink for this image: **https://unsplash.com/photos/-XGhtJXY-yY**

Ready?

Upload the **image**.

Press **Ctrl/Cmd+J** to *duplicate* the **image**.

Click on the **Adjustments icon** & *select* **Levels...**

Adjust **Black Level** slider to **12%** (see yellow rectangle) and the **Output Black Level** slider to **25%** (see red rectangle).

Click on the **red button** in the top left corner of the Levels pop-out window to close it.

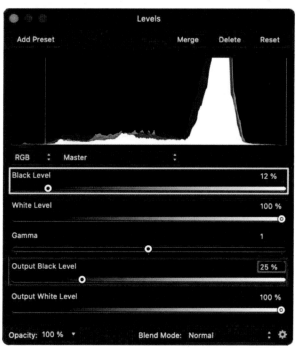

Go to the **Layers Panel** and *click* on the **top layer's checkmark** (see yellow square in the below image) to see the *before* & *after* effect.

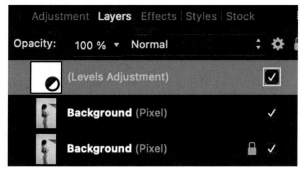

Which image do you prefer? Can you guess which one has been edited? We sure hope so :)

Would you like to see another effect we can add to this?

Click on the **Adjustments icon** & *select* **Black and White...**

Press the **red button** to *close* out this **pop-out window**. When you do this action, the image will look very washed out. It seems like a lot of details have been blasted away.

Let's experiment with the sliders in the Black and White adjustment's pop-out window and see what changes we can make. To do this:

Press **Ctrl/Cmd+J** to *duplicate* the **top Black & White layer**. This will create a second Black & White adjustment layer.

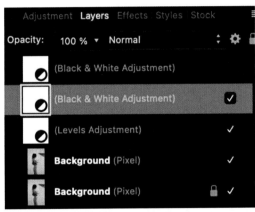

Uncheck the **top layer** & *click* on the **first Black & White layer** so it's highlighted in blue (see this image of our Layers Panel).

Double-click on this layer's **preview thumbnail** to reveal its pop-out window with its different Hue adjustment sliders (we added a yellow square around this so you know where it is).

Now, we will adjust the sliders to reveal the different parts of our model, her clothing, her background and even the shadows.

Adjust the **Red's** to **15%** to accentuate the model's lips.

Adjust the **Yellow's** to **15%** to accentuate the model's skin tone.

Leave the **Green's** alone.

Adjust the **Cyan** to **-45%** to add contrast to her white jacket.

Adjust the **Blues** to **60%** to add reveal the shadows better.

Adjust the **Magenta** to **107%** to even out some skin changes due to the above adjustments.

Click on the **red button** at the top-left of this pop-out window to close it.

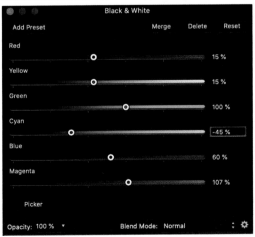

Check off the **current layer** & *check* on the **top layer** in the Layers Panel. This will show our image with just the Black & White adjustment.

Alternate *checking* **on** & **off** the top two Black & White adjustment layers to see the dramatic difference.

Done. Which do you like the best? Matte look in black and white or in color? It's a subtle effect.

Finished. This ends this short, but sweet tutorial.

Tutorial 5: How to do a Sky Replacement

In this tutorial, we are going to learn how do a sky replacement. That is, we're going to remove the sky in our first image and add a new image to replace it. Trust us, this will be fun. Please have the image named **Tutorial 5 - Mount Rushmore** & **Tutorial 5 - Sky** uploaded to your screen so we can begin. Here are the hyperlinks to these images on the web:

https://www.facebook.com/WritePublish/photos/a.351772392040734/353076735243633

https://pixabay.com/photos/nature-sky-night-stars-2609647/

With both of these images uploaded to Affinity Photo, we're going to start with the Mt. Rushmore image.

Select the **Selection Brush Tool.**

Select the **sky** by *clicking* on the **left-side of the sky** & *dragging* the **cursor** to the right and off the image's borders.

As you make your selection, you might miss parts of the rock face like we did (see yellow rectangle).

To correct this mistake:

Hold-down the **Option/Alt button** & *paint* over **the rock area** we want to correct from the starting point of underneath the rocks (not from above in the sky area). See this screenshot where we show you the two positions, we used our Selections Brush to click one-time in each position to move the selection line (i.e., the dancing ants) up to the border of the rocks & sky.

Hint: Every time you *hold down* the **Option/Alt key** and *use* a **Tool**, the opposite action will occur. This is what professionals use in our workflows. It makes our work incredibly faster.

With the selection now running along the rock face, let's make the selection even better.

Go to the **Toolbar** (horizontal area above the Contextual Toolbar) & *click* on the **Refine...** button.

Paint over the **top of the rockface** and when done, *press* **Apply** to *close* out the **Refine Selection pop-out window.**

This is where we used the Refine Selection brush (see the matte red brush line over the rock perimeter).

After we *pressed* **Apply**, the selection was much cleaner (notice how the dancing ants fit perfectly).

With the selection done as well as we can, let's continue:

Press **Ctrl/Cmd+J** to *duplicate* our **layer**.

Press **Ctrl/Cmd+D** to *deselect* out **selection** (e.g., the dancing ants).

Go to the **second image's tab** & and *press* **Ctrl/Cmd+C** to copy it.

Press **Ctrl/Cmd+C** to *copy* this **image**.

Go back to the **Mount Rushmore image** & *press* **Ctrl/Cmd+V** to *paste* the **stars image** on top of the Mount Rushmore image.

Let's change the name of the layers in the Layers Panel so we won't be confused as we work on them. Renaming layers is a simple and effect thing to do when working with multiple layers.

Double-click on the **top layer** & *type* in **"Sky"**.

Double-click on the **middle layer** & *type* **"MRM 2"** for Mount Rushmore 2.

Double-click on the **bottom layer** & *type* **"MRM 1"** for the original Mount Rushmore image.

When you've done each of these steps, this is what our Layers Panel should now look like:

Two things to note about Layers:

One: You can always tell what the original layer is because it'll have a Lock icon on it (see yellow square).

Two: Sometimes when you *double-click* a **layer** to rename it, the software program won't allow it for one or two tries. We don't know what it happens, but it does sometimes. Just do the operation again until you can rename the layer. It's what it is.

With the layers renamed...

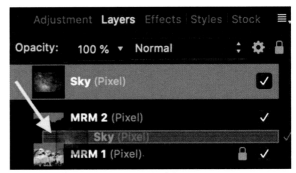

Click on the **Sky** layer & *drag* it **underneath-and-to-the-right** of the **MRM 2** layer.

This is a screenshot showing you this action. Notice how the left-side of the Sky layer is not all the way to the left as is being placed underneath the **MRM 2** layer.

Click on the **Sky layer** & *select* the **Move Tool** and *move* & *rescale* the **Sky image** wherever you want it. This image is showing you that we selected the Sky image's layer because it's blue.

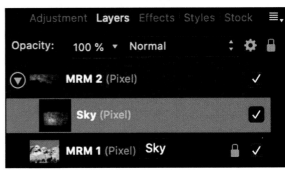

Note: To rescale an image *click* & *drag* on the **four corner nodes**. For us all we did was *click* & *drag* the **lower right corner node** to fill up the rest of this image.

Done. We've now done a sky replacement, but there's more to this than just taking one photo and adding to another. We need to now match the colors of both images together. Why? Because we want the composite image to look as natural as possible. Currently, the MRM image is in broad daylight while the Sky image was probably taken at night. So, we've got a bit work to do to blend these together.

Click on the **MRM 1** layer so it's highlighted in blue.

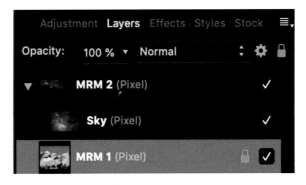

Remember: The most common mistake new users make when using Affinity Photo is that they forget to active the correct layer before continuing with their work.

Go to the **icons bar** and *click* on the **Adjustments icon** and *select* **Brightness and Contrast**... A pop-out window will appear. Make the following adjustments:

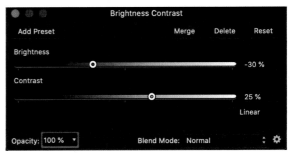

Brightness to **-30%**

Contrast to **25%**.

Click **anywhere on the canvas** to make this pop-out window disappear (or *press* the **red** button).

The colors aren't yet matched, so we've got one more adjustment to make:

Go again to the **icons bar** and *click* on the **Adjustments icon** and *select* **Lens Filter**...

This is what the **Lens Filter** pop-out window looks like. Notice how the default Filter Color is orange (see yellow rectangle).

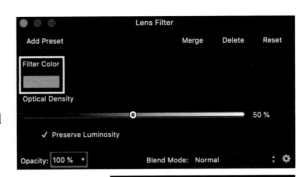

What we need to do is to *click* on this **orange rectangle** and when the Color Wheel pops out, we'll *change* the **color** to a dark blue. So...

Click on the **Filter Color rectangle...**

Move the **Hue node** to a dark blue. The Hue node is the small white circle on the outside ring that goes around the middle triangle - both parts make up the Color Wheel.

When you do this, notice how the Filter Color rectangle (see the yellow rectangle with the blue rectangle inside of it) also changes color to match the color we've chosen with the Color Wheel.

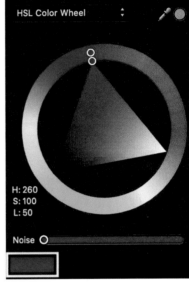

Click on the **Lens Filter pop-out window** and the Color Wheel will disappear. If your Lens Filter pop-out window disappears, do you remember how to make it reappear? **Answer**: You click on the Lens Filter Adjustment layer's white preview thumbnail.

Adjust the **Optical Density** slider to **65%**.

Close this **window** by either *pressing* the **red button** or *clicking* **anywhere on the canvas.**

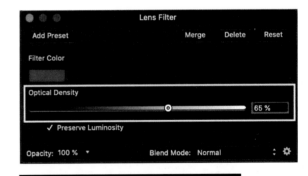

This is what our final Layers Panel should look like:

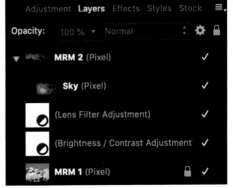

Done. This is our first final image.

Before we finish this tutorial, we want to show you another way you can colorize Mount Rushmore other than using the Lens Filter adjustment.

 Go to the **Layers Panel** & *uncheck* the **Lens Filter Adjustment layer**. This will deactivate that effect making it like it isn't even there.

 Click on the **MRM 1 layer** so it's highlighted in blue.

 Select the **Paint Brush Tool** (or *press* **B**).

 Go to the **Colors Studio** & *find* the **Color Picker Tool**. It looks like a water dropper.

Note: To use the Color Picker Tool, you need to click on it and while holding-down the left mouse button and then hover the cursor, which will look like a magnifying glass (see image below), over a color on your screen you want to pick (we chose a pink color from the Sky background). When you've found the color you want, release the mouse button. Then, go back to the Color Picker Tool's area & click once on the small circle to the right of the Color Picker Tool (see yellow square in bottom image). This final step will make the color on the Color Wheel the same color you chose using the Color Picker Tool's magnifying cursor. The next steps will tell you what to do.

 Click & *hold-down* the **Color Picker Tool** and *bring* it to a **portion of our image** where the color is the same we'd like to paint on top of the MRM image.

 Release the **mouse button** when you've found your color.

Go back to **where** the Color Picker Tool is located and *click* one-time on the **small circle** to its right (see small yellow square in this image). This will change the Hue color on the Color Wheel to match the color you chose using the Color Picker Tool.

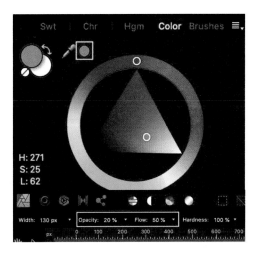

Now all we need to do is *paint* over the **MRM 1** layer to make its color the same as the color we chose using the Color Picker Tool. Normally, we need to change the Opacity of this color down to around 20% because the effect will be too drastic. So, let's do that.

Go to the **Contextual Toolbar** & *adjust* the **Opacity** to **20%** and *set* the **Flow** at **50%** (see yellow rectangle).

Note: Make sure just the bottom **MRM 1** layer is selected and highlighted in blue before you start painting.

Paint over the **MRM 1** image changing its color to the sky color we chose in the steps above. But make sure you only paint over the facade one time. Use the shortcut **Ctrl/Cmd+Z** to *undo* any **errors**.

Done. This is our second final image.

If you compare this image using this technique with the Paint Brush Tool, you'll see it's a bit more subdued and the image using the Lens Filter adjustment is a bit brighter.

Either way, the image is now finished. You need to decide which method you like best.

Note: We no longer need this image. So please remove it or save it before the next lesson.

Finished. This ends this tutorial.

The Color Wheel

This is a brief overview of the Color Wheel in case you didn't understand how it works. The outside ring represents the different colors (or more formally, Hues). The white node inside the inner triangle allows you to adjust the chosen Hue's Saturation and Luminosity (or Brightness).

So, every time you choose a new Hue, you can also change its appearance with the inner triangle.

In our latest book, The Affinity Designer Manual, we have a whole chapter on Color Theory, Modes, and Codes. If you want to do some self-learning on colors used in photo editing, we can suggest you do a search for "color theory in photo editing". It's a very involved topic, so be prepared for a steep learning curve.

When we first started using Affinity Photo, we did not know much about the different colors. Now that we do, we highly recommend you do further study on this matter.

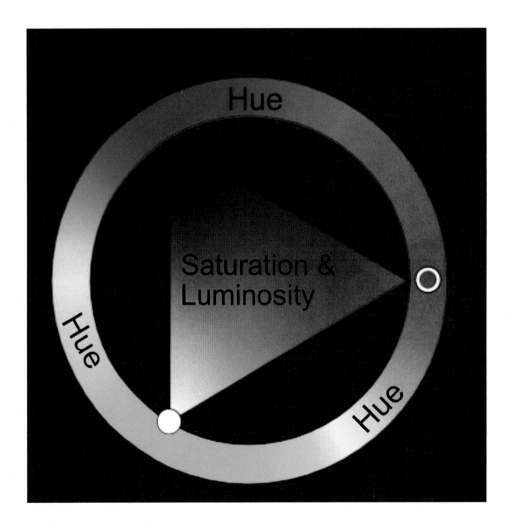

Special Offer: If you contact us, we'll send you the chapter on Color Theory, Modes, and Codes. This chapter teaches you all you need to know about how to properly use colors and why things like FF0000 is the Hue Red. All you have to do is request it.

Our email is Kuhlmanpublishing@yahoo.com

Tutorial 6: How to Create a High-Speed Effect

In this Affinity Photo tutorial, you are going to learn how to make a high-speed effect. Please have the image named **Tutorial 6 - Hallway** uploaded to your screen so we can begin. Here is the current hyperlink for this image is **https://pixabay.com/photos/architecture-building-infrastructure-2569760/**

Ready?

Once you have the image uploaded to the canvas, do this:

Press **Ctrl/Cmd+J** to *duplicate* the **image**.

Go to the **Menu bar - Filters - Blur - Zoom Blur...** A pop-out window will appear.

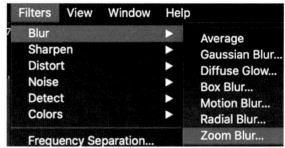

Adjust the **Radius** to **8 px**.

Press **Apply** when done. The higher the Radius the more blur effect you'll create.

Next, we need to apply a Mask layer to hide part of this layer that has the zoom blur applied.

To do this:

Click on the **top layer** so it's highlighted in blue.

Go to the **icons bar** and *click* on the **mask icon**.

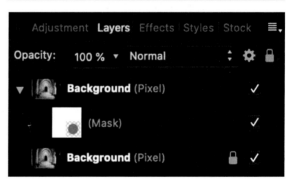

Select the **Paint Brush Tool** (or *press* **B**).

Press **X** if you need to *change* the Foreground colors. We want **black** (to reveal image below).

Note: When using Masks, like how we talked about in the Basics portion of this book, after you've applied a mask to an image you want to paint on it to reveal the layer(s) beneath, you have to paint in black. To hide the lower layer(s), you have to paint in white. If this is a concept that is hard for you to grasp, just know it was also very hard for us, too. It's just one of those things in life that you have to accept it just the way it is.

Go to the **Contextual Toolbar** & *adjust* these **values** to our Paint Brush Tool.

Width (the same as the height of the rear doorway)

Opacity: 100% (Shortcut is 0 when the Paint Brush Tool is active.

Flow: 100%.

Hardness: 0%.

Note: Your Width will most-likely not be the same size as ours. Just make sure the diameter of the Brush's circular cursor is the same height as the doorway and you'll be fine (see bottom image).

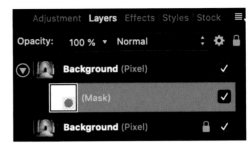

Important: Make sure the Mask layer is selected and highlighted in blue before continuing.

Position the Paint Brush Tool's **circular cursor** over the doorway & *click* **one-time**. This will remove the effects of the Zoom Blur in that one area of our image.

Here's a screenshot showing you the size of what your Paint Brush Tool's cursor should look like before you click on **it** (see white circle).

Done.

The image looks great and it only took a few steps to create the cool effect. Take a look at back hallway behind the back doorway. It's clear and in focus, whereas the rest of the image has the High-Speed effect added to it.

Finished. This ends this lesson.

Tutorial 7: How to Create a Dispersion Effect

This is a very creative tutorial and we hope you like it. We are still not masters of this technique but wanted to show you what we know and maybe you'll learn something and surpass our efforts. Please email us your work, we'd love to see it. Please have the image named **Tutorial 7 - Monk** uploaded to your screen so we can begin. Here is the current hyperlink to the image:

https://www.pexels.com/photo/selective-focus-photography-of-monk-during-meditation-2421467/

Ready?

Click on the **Selection Brush Tool** so it's active.

Make a **selection** of the monk.

Press **Ctrl/Cmd+J** <u>two times</u> so our image layer is duplicated twice.

Click & *drag* the **bottom-most layer** to the **Trashcan** on the icons bar.

Press **Ctrl/Cmd+D** to *deselect* the **dancing ants** (or the selection).

Click on the **top layer** so it's highlighted in blue.

Go to the **Toolbar** and *click* on the **Liquify Persona** (see yellow square).

Click & *drag* the **Monk's image to the right**. It will look weird (see this image).

Press **Apply** when done.

Note: When using the Liquify Persona, any adjustments you make the image takes time to master. For this lesson, plan on clicking & dragging 20 times to the right. If you feel you've made a mistake, simply press Ctrl/Cmd+Z to undo what you've done.

Like everything, practice makes perfect.

Go to the **Layers Panel** & *click* on the **top layer** so it's highlighted in blue (it should already be highlighted, but it's better to make sure).

Go to the **icons bar** and *click* on the **mask icon**.

Click on the Mask's **preview thumbnail** so just the mask layer is highlighted in blue.

Press **Ctrl/Cmd+I** to *invert* the **new mask layer**. You'll see its preview thumbnail is now covered with a thick black line. The image will have returned back to its original image.

We've placed a yellow square around the preview thumbnail. Notice how there is a thick vertical black line covering the image of the monk.

This preview thumbnail will look different from the mask we'll apply to the bottom layer. That mask will be white.

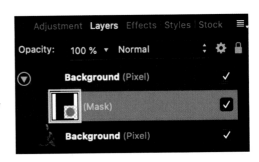

Click on the **bottom layer** so it's highlighted in blue.

Go to the **icons bar** and *click* on the **mask icon** to *create* a **new mask layer**.

Click again on the **bottom Mask's preview thumbnail** so it's highlighted in blue (see our image).

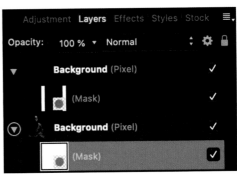

Select the **Paint Brush Tool**.

Go to the **Color Panel** & *click* on the **Brushes Tab**.

Change the **Type** to **Textures** & *select* **Grunge Pattern 05**. Make sure you click on this Brush type and it's highlighted in blue before continuing on with this lesson.

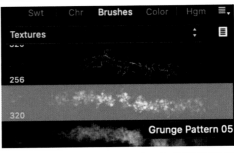

Click on the **Color Tab** & *set* the **Foreground** to *black*. Ours already was. If yours wasn't *press* the **X** key to alternate the Fore-/Background colors.

Note: When you paint in black, you will make the look like it's disintegrating a bit. The black paint on the mask removes the parts of the image you paint on revealing a transparent background.

Paint over the **right-side** of our monk. Feel free get as creative as you want.

Go to the **Contextual Toolbar** and *vary* the **size** of your Paint Brush's **Width**. The different sizes of disintegration paint strokes will make the effect look better.

Now, we want to bring back some of the monk we removed. To do this, we'll click on the top layer's mask preview thumbnail and paint in white.

Click on the **top layer's mask preview thumbnail**.

Change the **Foreground** color to **white** (or simply *press* **X**).

Paint over the **areas of the monk we've painted over** to remove parts of the monk, as well as paint to the right of the monk to create the right-going disintegration effect.

Go to the **Contextual Toolbar** and *change* the **Width** of your Paint Brush. The different sizes of disintegration paint strokes will make the effect look better.

Note: When you paint, don't click & drag the paint brush cursor. Instead make single mouse-clicks to bring back a portion of the disintegrated monk we use the Liquify Persona for.

Once you are done creating your dispersion effect using the paint brush strokes, we'll want to add a background to our photo. You are free to choose the color of your choosing. We will make our background color gray.

To do this:

Click on the **Rectangle Tool** and *click* & *drag* a **rectangle over the entire image**.

Click on the **top Rectangle layer** & *move* it to the **bottom** of the Layers Panel (see the yellow arrow for this action).

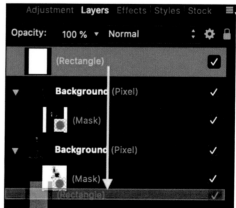

73

Click on the **bottom rectangle layer** so it's highlighted in blue.

Go to the **Color Studio** & *move* the **inner Saturation/Luminosity node** halfway up to make its color gray (see yellow arrow for this action).

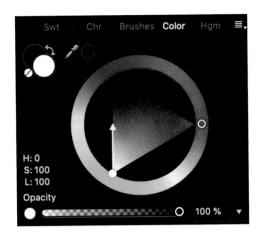

Done. This is our final image.

Note: We are done using this image. Please save your work or delete it with Ctrl/Cmd+W.

Finished. This ends this tutorial.

Tutorial 8: How to Create a Face Warp

In this tutorial, we are going to learn how to create a funny face warp. We'll show you how to get started, but the actual doing of the face work is up to you. Please have the image named **Tutorial 8 - Model** uploaded to your screen so we can begin. Here is the current hyperlink to the image:

https://pixabay.com/photos/model-female-girl-beautiful-woman-429733/

Ready?

Open the **image** onto the canvas.

Press **Ctrl/Cmd+J** to *duplicate* our **image**.

Click on the **Liquify Persona** and *click* on **Apply**.

Look to the right of the User Interface (UI) and see the three vertical panels **Mesh/Histogram, Brush/Navigator, Mask, & History/Channels**.

In the Mesh/Histogram panel:

Uncheck the **Show Mesh button**. We don't need to see this to do our technique.

In the Brush/Navigator panel:

Press **Ctrl/Cmd+0** (zero) to *fit* our image into the screen. For this step, make sure your Affinity Photo screen is maximized on your computer's screen.

Move the **Size** to **350 px**.

Move the **Hardness slider** all the way to the left so its value is **0%**.

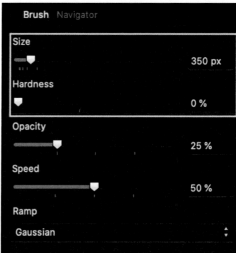

Now, we can begin warping her face.

Click on her **hair** over her left eye (our right side) & *move* **it** to the right side and away from her eye.

Note: This action of warping this image is exactly the same mouse cursor movements as the previous tutorial. Take your time and click on the hair and move it just a bit to the right.

This is what we've done:

Go to where the Tools normally are (left side of the screen) and click on the **Liquify Pinch Tool** (see darkened tool in this screenshot). This will allow us to make things bigger just by *clicking* & *holding* the **mouse button**.

Go back to the **Brush/Navigator panel** on the right side of the screen and *set* the **Speed** to **100** (see yellow rectangle).

This will allow us to use this Tool in a much faster fashion.

Click **one time** on the woman's right eye (our left side) so the Liquify Pinch Tool's circular cursor appears. Once it does, as we just click & hold the eye will warp outwards.

Hold **as long as you want** to *create* the **image of your dreams**.

Note: If you hold-down the Opt/Alt button, the effect will reverse and instead of enlarging it'll shrink.

Click & *hold* the **mouse button** over the **mouth** and the **nose** to your liking. It doesn't matter how your image looks in comparison to ours.

Done. This is our final image. The bug woman, herself.

Finished. This ends this creative and funny tutorial.

Tutorial 9: How to Create a Beautiful Pop Art Effect

In this lesson, we're going to learn how to make a beautiful pop art effect. This is an artistic effect and we hope you like it. We'll also be adding texture to the final image, so that's another skill you'll learn now, too. Please have the images named **Tutorial 9 - Woman** & **Tutorial 9 - Stone** uploaded to your screen so we can begin. Here are their current hyperlinks to the images:

https://pixabay.com/photos/woman-model-young-model-fashion-2381628/

https://pixabay.com/photos/kennedy-stone-background-ground-3740228/

Ready?

We'll start with the image of the woman. Have that in front of you so we can begin.

Click on the **Adjustments icon** & *select* **Threshold**.

Adjust the **Threshold** slider to **40%.**

Exit out of the **pop-out window** by *pressing* the **red X**.

Note: Using the **Threshold** adjustment makes the image **black** & **white**. Moving the slider to the right & left changes the image.

      0% makes the image entirely **white**.   **100%** makes the image entirely **black**.

For this effect, we want to make it so the woman is the only thing that's **black** in this entire picture, and everything else is **white**.

That means, everything surrounding her needs to be *painted* **white**.

To do this:

Select the **top layer** so that it's highlighted in blue. Ours already is.

Click on **Add Pixel Layer** (located next to the **Trashcan**).

Select the **Paint Brush Tool** (or *press* **B**). Make sure you've changed the Paint Brush back to a Basic brush. If not, go to the Brushes Tab in the Colors Studio and click on the types of brushes drop-down menu (see yellow rectangle) and *select* **Basic**.

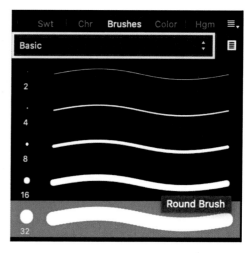

Press **X** to *change* the **Foreground** color to **white** (see Color Panel to check if the **white** circle is on top of the **black** circle - **X** is the keyboard shortcut to switch these two Fore-/Background colors).

Go to the **Contextual Toolbar** and *set* the **Hardness** to **100**%.

Adjust the **Width** of the brush to about the 1/3 the height of the woman.

Paint in **white** to cover the lower object she is standing on. Take your time and do a good job. If you make any mistakes, simply *press* **Ctrl/Cmd+Z** to *undo* your **error**.

Press **Ctrl/Cmd + 0** (zero) when you're done to see the entire picture on your canvas. This image to the right is what our image looks like after we've painted away all of the bottom black areas.

We are halfway done. Next, we want to add some color to the image.

To do this, we'll be adding a Gradient Map.

Go to the **icons bar** and click on the **Adjustments icon** & *select* **Gradient Map**... In the pop-out window you will see the color bar colored **Red** - **Green** - **Blue** (with different shades in-between).

Here, you need to look at the line going through the colors and the three circles on it. We want to delete the **green** circle. To do this, *click* on the **green** circle (see the **black** square) and *press* the **Delete** button that's inside the pop-out window (see white rectangle).

Now, we want to **Reverse** the Gradient.

Press the **Reverse** button underneath the **Delete** button (see image above). This will change the places of the **reds** & **blues** in the image.

Note: To save space, our images are not the entire image as we have it on our canvas.

The **Gradient Map** has made it so everything that was **black** in our picture has now become **blue**, and everything that was **white** has become **red**. If we want to, we can change these colors. We personally like the red/blue look, but for practice we'll change the <u>red to a hot pink</u> and the <u>blue to black</u>.

Click on **preview thumbnail** on the top Gradient Map layer and the pop-out window will reappear.

Click on the **right red node** (see white square) so it's larger than the blue node.

Click on the **Color Box** (see the green rectangle) and the Color Wheel will pop-out.

Move the **Hue node** to the <u>hot pink color</u> (see the curved yellow arrow for this action).

Let's *change* the **blue** color to a black.

Click on the **left blue node** (white square) so it's larger than the pink node.

Click on the **Color Box** (green rectangle) and the Color Wheel will pop-out.

Move the Color Wheel's **inside node** straight down to make to black (yellow arrow).

Press the **red X** to *close* these **windows**.

Our pop art effect is just about done. As a finishing touch though, let's add a little bit of texture to our picture

Click on the **tab** for the second image for this tutorial - the stone. If it's not yet uploaded, pls do it now.

With the Granite image in front of you...

Press **Ctrl/Cmd + C** to copy it.

Click again on the **image** of the woman.

Press **Ctrl/Cmd + V** to *paste* the **granite image** on top of it.

Select the **Move Tool** (or *press* **V**) and *resize* the **granite image** so that it's covering the entire picture.

Then we're going to change this granite's **Opacity** from **100%** to **10%**. You will see the woman under the granite layer. This has now added a nice little bit of texture to our image.

Hint: To change the Opacity of a layer, simply have that layer selected and press 1 for 10%, 5 for 50% and 0 for 100% Opacity.

Done. This is what our image looks like now. If you wanted to crop it, go ahead, but we like it just as it is.

Finished. This ends this lesson. We hope you enjoyed it.

Tutorial 10: How to Create a Pop Out or 3D Effect

Creating 3D effects that make it look like different cool objects are literally coming out of computer and smartphones is a favorite edit of most photo editors. The limits of creativity are limitless. In this fun tutorial, we'll be making a horse jump out of a laptop's screen.

Before we get started, please open your image folder, and have these images uploaded to your screen as separate tabs: **Tutorial 10 - Horse**, **- Laptop**, **-Path**. Here are their current hyperlinks:

https://pixabay.com/photos/horse-horseback-riding-721136/

https://pixabay.com/de/photos/macbook-luft-laptop-apfel-stift-2628552/

https://upload.wikimedia.org/wikipedia/commons/1/10/Scenic-dirt-road-in-spring_%28Unsplash%29.jpg

This is the final image we'll be creating. We think it looks impressive.

This tutorial has four parts:

Part I: Make the screen of the laptop transparent.

Part II: Make a selection of the top part of horse that is clearing the hurdle.

Part III: Import the Path image onto the laptop's image.

Part IV: Import the selected horse image and place it in the computer screen to finish the effect.

Part I: Make the screen of the laptop transparent. Please have the image of the laptop in front of you.

Click on the **Pen Tool** and then *go* to the **Contextual Toolbar** and *click* on the first **Mode** (see yellow rectangle). This is called the Pen Mode.

For this part of this lesson, what we need to do is to use the Pen Tool and create four nodes at the four corners of the screen just outside the screen itself. We don't want our lines created by the four nodes to come too close to the screen, nor do we want to have the lines inside the screen. This is because after we have used the Pen Tool to make this selection, we will cut out the screen area and make it transparent. We make it transparent so we can add any picture inside of it that we want to.

Take a look at this image. Think to yourself which lines (or nodes) are done correctly, and which are not.

Answer: **Node 1** is too close to the screen, which makes its line (8) it shares with **Node 7** go over the screen area.

To fix this:

Click on the **Node Tool** and *click & drag* **nodes 1 & 7** a bit further away from the screen's corners. Make sure line 8 is outside the screen area like lines 2, 4, 6 already are. Is there any other part of our screen image that could be worked on?

Maybe line 4 is a bit too high off the screen. To fix this, again use the Node Tool and lower the Nodes 3 & 5 just a bit. But, for this lesson, Line 4 is ok where it is.

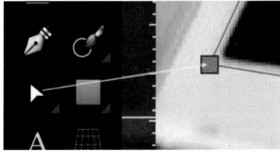

With the lines completed, all we need to do is *go* to the **Contextual Toolbar** & *click* on **Selection**. This will create a selection of the screen we just used the Pen Tool with.

Note: If you skip this step, the technique will not work. Whenever you "make a selection" you will see the typical 'dancing ants' move around the selection. Make sure you see these 'ants' after you've pressed **Selection**.

Because the selection we made is directly in the middle of our image, we need to *invert* our **pixel selection** so it differentiates itself from the whole of the image.

Go to the **Menu bar - Select - Invert Pixel Selection**.

Note: When you invert the pixel selection, you'll see that the dancing ants have attached themselves to at least one of the four borders of the image.

81

Most of the time, these adhere to only one side, but in this tutorial, the dancing ants decided to adhere to three of the four sides.

Go to the **icons bar** and *click* on the **mask icon** (see yellow square). This will remove the screen area and make it transparent.

Press **Crtl/Cmd+D** to *deselect* the **dancing ants**.

This is what our image looks like now.

This ends Part I of this lesson. Next, we'll be working on the image of the horse. Please go ahead and switch photos so the horse image is on your screen.

Part II: Make a selection of the top part of horse that is clearing the hurdle.

Click on the **image tab** named **Tutorial 10 - Horse**.jpg so the horse image is in front of us.

Click on the **Selection Brush Tool** and then go to its Contextual Toolbar and make these changes:

1. *Adjust* the **Width** to about the size of the <u>horse's left foot</u>.

2. *Check* on **Snap to edges** (see yellow rectangle).

3. *Set* the **Mode** to **Add** (see left side of this image).

Click & *drag* a **selection** over the horse and woman for the parts that are <u>above the hurdle</u>.

Note: The yellow arrows represent areas of the horse image that the Selection Brush missed. Because of this, we'll need to use the Refine Selection Tool located on the Contextual Toolbar.

Do you see any other areas of the horse we missed?

Answer: If you noticed the shadowed area directly underneath the horse's left hoof, you'd be correct. We'll address this area soon.

Go to the **Contextual Toolbar** & *click* on **Refine...** to *refine* the **missed areas** our Selection Brush missed.

Here is a screenshot of where we painted over our image. You should do the same. It isn't important to paint over the entire horse with one click & drag like we did. We only did it this way to be able to show you where we used the Refine Selection Brush in one image. Normally, we will paint over small sections of our subject.

After we *pressed* **Apply** in the pop-out window for the Refine Selection Brush, we were shown what our image looked like afterwards.

If you look closely at your image after you've pressed Apply, you will notice that there are some dancing ants inside your woman's & horse's bodies. To remove these glitches, simply hover your cursor over these spots and click once with you mouse. This will remove these leftover 'ants'.

To illustrate what we mean, we've added white circles to the image to mimic the Selection Brush Tool that is already activated. These are the areas on our woman/horse that have these leftover 'ants'. By clicking one-time in the areas of our white circles, these 'ants' will disappear.

Note: When using the one-click method near the border of the image (see woman's helmet and lower back), make sure the inside of the brush's cursor not touching the dancing ants. This will cause the selection to be skewed.

Yellow Circle Note: After you've used the Refine Selection tool and have one-clicked away the annoying leftover ants, to remove portions of the selections all you need to do is hold-down the Option/Alt button and click one-time where the yellow circle is (again, it represents the Width of your Selection Brush Tool). When you hold down the Option/Alt button and click, you're telling Affinity Photo that you want to do the opposite of what your chosen tool normally does.

Pro Tip: Using the **Option/Alt button** while working on photos greatly increases your workflow speed.

This is what our selection looks like now after these tweaks we did on the previous page. Much cleaner!

Now, we want to remove the background from our image so everything will be transparent. With that image, we can simply copy & past it onto our laptop image and fit it inside the screen.

We'll remove the background in a similar fashion we used for the laptop image.

Go to the **icons bar** and *click* on the **mask icon**. This will make everything not selected disappear into transparency.

Press **Ctrl/Cmd+D** to *deselect* the **dancing ants**.

This is the image you should have on our screen:

That's the end of Part II. This is the image we'll be placing inside the laptop screen to finish out 3D effect.

Part III: Import the Path image onto the laptop's image.

This step is simple.

Click on the **Path image's tab** so the image is in front of you.

Press **Ctrl/Cmd+C** anywhere on the canvas to *copy* this **image**.

Go to the **Laptop image's tab** and *press* **Ctrl/Cmd+V** to *paste* the **Path's image** on top of the laptop image.

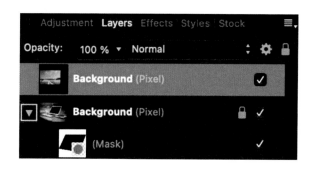

This is what the Layers Panel should look like now. We placed a small yellow square over the icon that represents a group. Currently the group is open because you can see the two layers that make it a group. If you clicked on the group icon (yellow square), the group would minimize itself and, on its layer, would be two preview thumbnails.

Click on the **group icon** to minimize its layers.

Click & *drag* the **top layer** beneath the grouped layer. See this screenshot for what your Layers Panel should now look like.

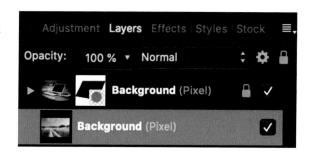

When we do this action, the path image's layer will be in the laptop's screen. We need to resize the path image so it fits perfectly "inside" the laptop.

Click & *drag* on the **corner blue nodes** to *resize* and *reposition* the **path image** so it looks perfect in the laptop's screen. See this image as a guide for you.

We are done with Part III.

Part IV: Import the selected horse image and place it in the computer screen to finish the effect. This last part is very similar to Part III. Ready?

Click on the **horse image's tab** with its transparent background.

Click on the **top layer** in the Layers Panel so it's highlighted in blue. This is a very important step!

Stop! Did you remember to do the last step? If you didn't the effect won't work and you'll get super frustrated.

Press **Ctrl/Cmd+C** to *copy* it.

Go to the **laptop image's tab** & *press* **Ctrl/Cmd+V** to *paste* the **horse's image** on top of the other images.

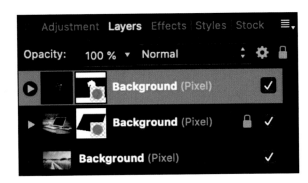

Move the **horse's layer** to the top of the Layers stack - if it isn't already there. This is what your Layers Panel should look like now.

The tutorial is almost completed: All we need to do now is adjust the positioning of the field and the horse.

We'll start with the horse.

Click on the **Move Tool** (or *press* **V**) to *resize* & *reposition* the **image of the horse**. This is where we've moved ours. Try to match what we have.

Note: If you wanted to quicken this technique, simply align the flat area of the horse along the lower portion of the laptop's screen. Do that and you're done.

Assuming you didn't do that...we need to remove the parts of the horse that's covering the outside of the laptop. To do this, we'll use the Erase Brush Tool.

Note: When using any brush in Affinity Photo you can paint precise straight lines by clicking one-time in one position and then holding-down the Shift key press the mouse button one-time and the brush will affect the area between you two mouse clicks in a perfectly straight line. We will use this brush technique now.

Click on the **Erase Brush Tool** & *click* **one-time** right below the left-bottom corner of the laptop's screen. Now, as you move the cursor to the right where the horse's legs are covering the laptop, the Erase Brush Tool will reveal what's hidden by the horse.

While this method is one of our favorites, there's a more precise way to remove the horse's image from the laptop.

Make sure the top horse layer is highlighted in blue before you do this next step.

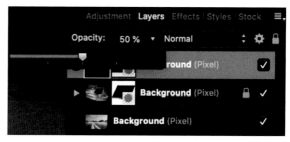

Click on the **Opacity slider** & *reduce* the **Opacity** of the horse's layer to **50%**. This will allow us to use Erase Brush Tool with greater precision (the lower image shows this change in Opacity).

We've marked out image with a yellow rectangle to show you the precision we could have in using the shift-erase-in-a-straight-line technique.

Now, with the edge of the horse/screen done, we can use freehand to use the Erase Brush Tool to remove the rest of the horse from in front of the laptop.

When you are done painting away the horse, don't forget to click make the Opacity 100% when done.

Note: When Opacity is selected, if you press 0 (zero), the Opacity will change to 100% and if you press 5, the Opacity will change to 50%.

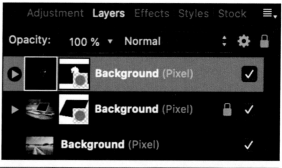

This is final Layers Panel (notice how the Opacity is back to 100%).

As a final touch, we *clicked* on our **Path layer** to *resize* & *reposition* **it** to fit what we personally prefer. Feel free to manipulate yours however you want.

Done. This is our final image.

Finished. This ends this tutorial.

Tutorial 11: How to Create a Water Flame Candle

Are you ready for a cool technique where we'll transform a normal-looking candle into a water flame candle. We'll use several already-learnt skills to pull this effect off and this tutorial should be a good re-enforcer of the skills you've learnt in this book so far.

Before we get started, please open your image folder, and have these images uploaded to your screen as separate tabs: **Tutorial 11 - Candle** & **Tutorial 11 - Water**. Here are their current hyperlinks:

https://www.facebook.com/WritePublish/photos/a.351772392040734/353084908576149

https://pixabay.com/de/illustrations/wasser-spritzen-png-2748695/

Once these images have been uploaded to Affinity Photo, let's...

Click on the **Water** image and *press* **Ctrl/Cmd+C** (to *copy*).

Click on the **Candle** image and *press* **Ctrl/Cmd+V** (to *paste* **it** on top of the Candle image).

Select the **Move Tool** (or *press* **V**) to *resize* & *move* the **water image** on top of the candle (left image).

Click on the **top white node** & *turn* the **water image** 90° counterclockwise (right image).

Now, we want to *flip* the **water image** so it'll look better as a water flame.

Using the **Move Tool**, *click* on the **water image** and *right-click* your **mouse**.

Choose **Transform - Flip Horizontal**.

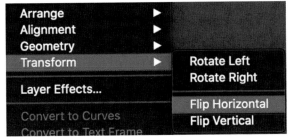

88

To make the flame look even more realistic, we need to remove some of the excess water we don't need.

To do this:

Click on the **top layer** so that the **water Background** is highlighted in blue - it should be already.

Go to the **icons bar** and *click* on the **mask layer icon**.

Click on the **preview thumbnail** on the mask layer so the Mask layer is highlighted in blue (see this image).

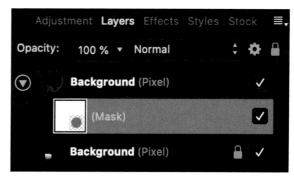

Select the **Paint Brush Tool** (or *press* **B**).

Set the **Foreground** color to **black** (use the shortcut X to alternate between the white & black Foreground positions). If it's already black, don't do anything.

Go to the **Contextual Toolbar** and *set* the **Hardness** to **0%**.

Paint over the **right side of the water image** so only the flat part remains (see this image).

With the wick going to the right and the water image going in the opposite direction, maybe we should switch the water image again.

Click on the **top layer** so it and the mask layer are highlighted in blue.

Click on the **Move Tool** (or *press* **V**).

Note: In order to perform a Transform action, the subject you want to transform needs to be selected with the Move Tool. If you don't do this, the transform action won't work.

Click on the **water image**, which is over the candle. Immediately, the Move Tool nodes will surround the water image.

Right-click on the **water** and *choose* **Transform - Flip Horizontal**.

Now, we're just going to paint away some of the water image we don't need for the image we want to create and to make it look as realistic as we can make it.

To do this:

Click on the **preview thumbnail** on the Mask layer so only the Mask layer is highlighted in blue. We do not want both top layers selected. Only the Mask's layer.

Press **B** for the **Paint Brush Tool**. Our brush settings are this: Opacity & Flow 100%, Hardness 0%.

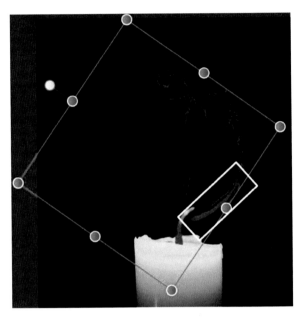

Set the **Foreground** color to **black**.

Paint carefully over **some of the bottom of the water** to make it look like the water flame starts someplace in the air (like a real flame would).

Optional: *Click* the **X key** to *change* the **Foreground** to **white** and *paint back in* **some of the water image** (see yellow rectangle for where we did this action.

Click again on the **top layer** in the Layers Panel so it's active.

Select the **Move Tool** again to *rotate* & *reposition* the **newly changed water** over the candle's wick. Look at where our white rotational node is located in this screenshot.

Now that we have the flame where we want it, let's change the candle's color to more of an **aqua-blue**.

To do this:

Click on the **Adjustments icon** & *select* **Recolor**.

Adjust the **Hue** to **190** & the **Saturation** to about **25%**.

Click on the **red button** to *close* this **pop-out window**.

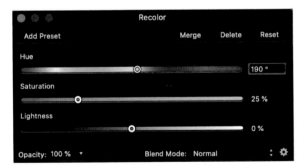

Using the **Recolor Adjustment** has affected the entire image, but we only wanted to change the color of the candle. So, we need to move the top **Recolor Adjustment** layer so that it's below-and-to-the-right of the bottom candle layer. When you make this change, you will see that the candle's color stays the same while the water image's color will go back to **blue**.

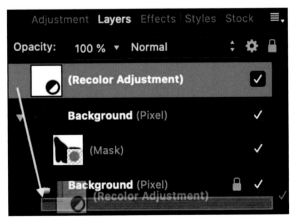

Click & *drag* the **top Recolor layer** below-and-to-the-right of the bottom Background layer (see yellow arrow for this action and necessary positioning).

Note: Layers in this position are called child layers because they only affect the layer they're attached too, and no other layer in the Layers Panel.

The last thing we're going to do is add a light to our image to make it look like this candle is shining.

To do this you have to:

Click anywhere in the **canvas area** so that none of the layers are highlighted in blue.

Go to the **Menu bar - Layer - New Live Filter Layer - Lighting**... We could have clicked on the Live Filters icon on the icons bar, but we wanted to show you another location for this action.

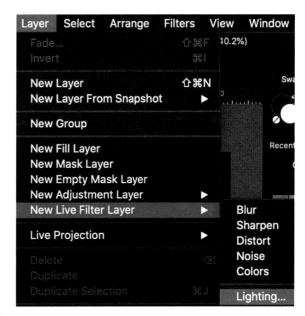

Note: Since none of the layers were highlighted in blue, the Lighting filter goes to the top of the Layers Panel. This is what we want.

In the new pop-out window, there are many very useful things we can adjust to enhance our image. But all we really want to do is add a glow to the middle of the candle's wick.

To add a glow to a specific place, we need to:

Change the **Type** of **Live Lighting** from **Spot** to **Point** (see blue-highlighted button).

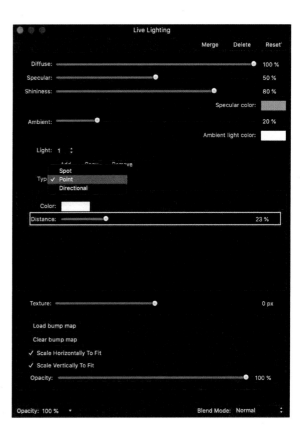

Adjust the **Distance** so the mid-point is in the middle of the wick and the circle just touches the outside of the water image's edge. Perhaps the effect will be too bright.

Note: We placed the below image where it is on this page because the hidden information on the right image isn't important to this edit.

If it's too bright, we can *click* on the **Specular Color** rectangle (see yellow rectangle) and *change* the **glow color** from a **white** to a soft **blue**.

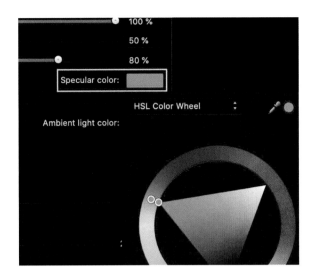

Click on the **Specular color rectangle** and immediately the Color Wheel will appear.

Move the **outside Hue node** to a nice soft blue color.

Press the **red button** in the top-left corner of the Live Lighting pop-out window to close it. It may not turn red until you hover your cursor over its icon.

Click **anywhere on the canvas** to make the blue nodes surround the image to disappear.

Done. This is the final image.

Finished. This ends this tutorial.

Tutorial 12: How to Create a Face Swap

This technique is funny one. It's where you take someone's face and implant it onto another's - always a classic. Before we get started, please open your image folder, and have these two images uploaded to your screen as separate tabs: **Tutorial 12 - Girls** & **Tutorial 12 - Baby**. We'll work with the baby image first.

Here are their current hyperlinks:

https://pixabay.com/de/photos/mädchen-jung-freunde-lächelnd-524239/

https://www.pexels.com/photo/baby-child-close-up-crying-47090/

The image of the baby's face should be in front of you now.

Select the **Free hand Selection Tool** (looks like a Lasso).

Draw a **selection** around the baby face - just above his eyebrows and down to his chin.

Go to the **Contextual Toolbar** and *click* on the **Refine button**.

When the Refine Selection pop-out window opens, we're just going to make one adjustment.

Move the **Feather slider** all the way to the right so its value is **100%**. This will make the edges of the selection the fuzziest possible.

Press the **Apply** button when done.

We are now going to *copy* this **image** of the baby's face & *paste* it on top of the image of the two girls.

Click on the **Move Tool** and then *press* **Ctrl/Cmd+C**.

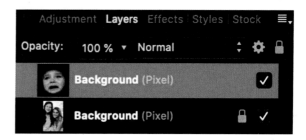

Click on the **tab** with the girls image.

Press **Ctrl/Cmd+V** (to *paste*).

Note: Make sure the top layer is active and highlighted.

Press the **8 key** on your keyboard to change this layer's Opacity to 80%. This way we can partially see through the baby's face to the girls image. We do this so we can more perfectly combine the images together.

Select the **Move Tool** (or *press* **V**).

Move the **baby's face** over the face of the girl on the right so the eyes line up.

Resize & *rotate* the **baby's face** by using the **blue nodes** around his face (see this image for comparison).

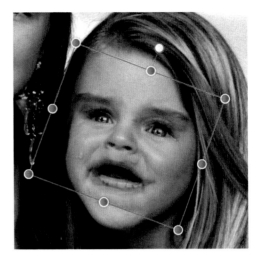

Change the **Opacity** to **100%** (by *pressing* **0** or by *clicking* on the **%** in the value box & *dragging* the **slider** all the way to the right).

The result:

The image could look better because the image of the baby's face isn't blending into the girl's face as well as we'd like it to look.

In this next part, we are going to make the blending of these two images match as well as we can make them.

To match the skin tones:

Go to the **icons bar** and *click* on the **Adjustments icon** and then *select* **HSL...**

Note: We only want the HSL Adjustment to affect the image of baby, so we need to move this new top layer down-and-to-the-right of the baby's face layer.

Click & *drag* the **HSL layer** below-and-to-the-right of the middle background layer (see image for action).

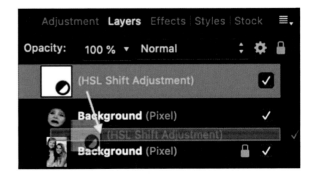

Your Layers Panel should now look like this.

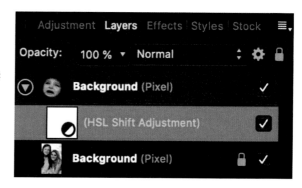

We now need to see the **HSL** pop-out window again. To make it reappear (if it's gone), simply *double-click* on its **preview thumbnail**.

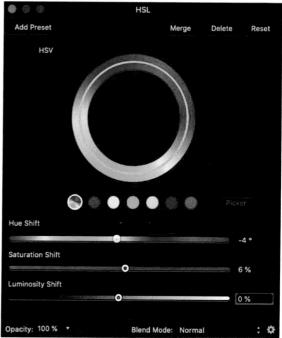

Once you have the HSL pop-out window open, these are the adjustments we recommend:

Slide the **Hue** slider to **-4°**, then *click* the **Tab key** to go to the next lower value box.

Bring the **Saturation Shift** to **6%**, then **press** the **Return key**.

Click on the **red button** in the top-left area of this pop-out window to close it.

Now, we need to *change* **the way the chin is blending in with the background image.**

To do this:

Click on the **baby's face layer** so it's selected.

Click on the **blue nodes** around the face in the image and make the face a little longer vertically. This action is tiny - like one or two millimeters. We added a yellow arrow to show you this action.

If the baby's face is bleeding off the girl's face, we are going to apply a **Mask**. When we paint to remove the girl's face, all we want to do is to gently paint over the area of the chin where there's a definite line. To do this:

Go to the **icons bar** and *click* on the **mask icon**.

Select the **Paint Brush Tool** (or *press* **B**).

Make sure your **Foreground** is **black** (use the **X** to switch, if necessary).

Go to the **Contextual Toolbar** & *set* these values: **Opacity** to **50%**, **Flow** to **100%**, **Hardness** to **0%**.

Adjust the **Width** of the Brush to about the <u>diameter of the child's eyes</u>.

Paint around **edges** of the baby's face.

Check out these before & after images. We enlarged them so you can more easily see the differences.

Before

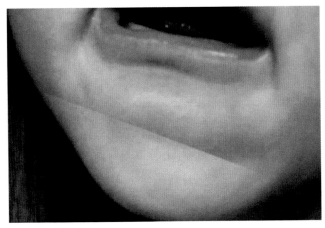

After

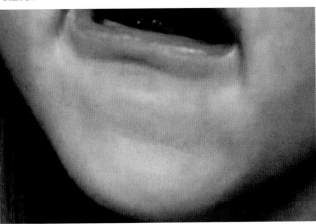

Done. This is our final image.

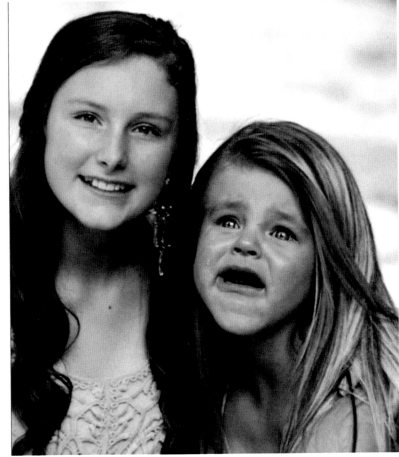

Finished. This ends this funny tutorial.

Tutorial 13: How to Crop an Image in a Circle Shape

Cropping images in different shapes is a creative way to create creative photo albums and collages, or to create family greeting cards. In this tutorial, we'll show you how to crop images in circle shapes, but you can also use what you learn here and crop in other shapes as well. The heart shape comes to mind for family cards for Valentine's Day, for example. Please have these images uploaded so we can begin: **Tutorial 13 - Woman** & **Tutorial 13 - Vase**. Here are the current hyperlinks:

https://pixabay.com/photos/guitar-beautiful-music-instrument-944262/

https://pixabay.com/photos/sunflower-vase-vintage-retro-wall-3292932/

Once you have the image of the woman uploaded onto the canvas, here's how you start (we'll use the sunflower image at the end of this tutorial to show you how you can add your newly cropped image with another image):

Let's start:

Click on the **small triangle menu icon** (yellow square) on the Rectangle Tool and in the pop-out window *select* the **Ellipse Tool**. Ignore this if it's already the Ellipse that's active.

Position the **cursor** <u>over the woman's nose</u> and *hold down* these keys (**Shift** + **Ctrl/Cmd**) as you click & *drag* a **perfect circle** over the woman's face and shoulders.

Press the **5 key** to instantly change the Ellipse's Opacity to 50%. Now *reposition* the **circle** where you want it.

Press the **0 key** to *change* the **Opacity** back to **100%** - when you are done positioning the circle.

The next step is a bit redundant, but necessary. We need to move the Background layer below-and-to-the-right of the Ellipse layer, but the only way we know to do this is to first move the top Ellipse layer below the Background layer and then after that's done move the Background layer below-and-to-the-right of the Ellipse layer. If you know how to do this another way, please tell us.

Click & *drag* the **Ellipse layer** beneath the Background layer. Then *click* & *drag* the **Background layer** below-and-to-the-right of the Ellipse layer

This is what your Layers Panel needs to look like after these changes.

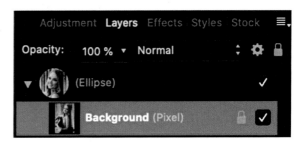

97

This is what our image should now look like.

We now have our image just the way we want it. But we need to save our image as a .png file so that we can use this image wherever we want for current or future projects. Saving it as a .png file will keep the transparency in this image. If you don't know what that means, just follow along and we'll show you what we mean in a few steps from now.

To export our image as a **.png** file...

   Go to the **Menu bar - File - Export**... (a pop-out window will appear with many choices).

Yellow: Normally, when you export images, they will be exported as JPEG's. So, this tab is usually selected with different, but similar options. You can tell the PNG tab is selected because it looks different from the other tabs.

Red: These are the dimensions of the image we want to export. If you click on one of these values to increase the Size, the other value will also increase. The Size of the image is reflected in the next marked area.

White: This is the size of the file you are about to send, which is directly related to the Red-marked values.

Green: Press this button when you're done making any changes to this screen.

   Save the **file** on your Desktop or in any folder of your choosing. We created one called **How to Crop an Image in a Circle Shape**.

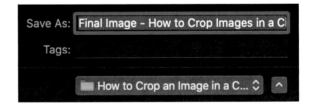

Note: Our image is now saved as a .png file, which means we can add it to any photo we want to create things like collages, greeting cards, etc. We recommend you also try this tutorial using the Heart Tool to create a similar effect.

With our current image in front of us...

Click **anywhere on the image** (transparent area or inside the circle) & *press* **Ctrl/Cmd+C** to *copy* it.

Click on the **Vase tab** so it's in front of us on the canvas.

Press **Ctrl/Cmd+V** to *paste* our **circle shape** on top of this new image.

Select the **Move Tool** & *reposition* the **woman** on the right-side of the sunflower image. Once you've found a good spot, we are now done.

Done. This is our final image.

Finished. This ends this tutorial.

Tutorial 14: How to Make a Realistic Shadow

Making shadows is a very important and subtle effect all good photo editors know how to do. There's nothing worse than adding an object to a photo and not take into account whether that object should be casting a shadow or not. When newly added objects to a photo don't have perfect shadows, as you'd expect in real life, it's very obvious a photo has been manipulated. Master photo editors are so good at shadows and subtle alternations, you can't tell the original from the manufactured.

Please have the image named **Tutorial 14 - Burger** uploaded to your screen. Here is the hyperlink:

https://pixabay.com/photos/burger-hamburger-food-lunch-meat-2018627/

Ready?

Select the **Selection Brush Tool** (looks like a paint brush with a dotted circle at its tip).

Paint a **selection** across the cheeseburger, so the dancing ants surround it.

When you make selections of objects like this burger that have minute details around its perimeter, we often times have to use the Refine Selection Tool so the software can make a more refined selection than we can do with a brush.

Go to the center of the **Contextual Toolbar** & *click* on **Refine...**

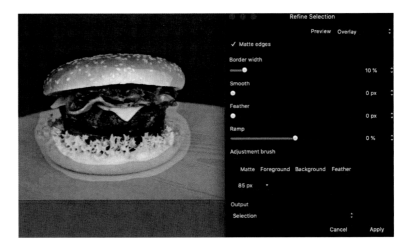

Paint a **selection** with the Refine Selection Brush (important that our burger is in full color while the background is Matt Red).

Press **Apply** when done.

Press **Ctrl/Cmd+J** <u>twice</u> to *duplicate* this **layer**.

Press **Ctrl/Cmd+D** to *deselect* the **selection**.

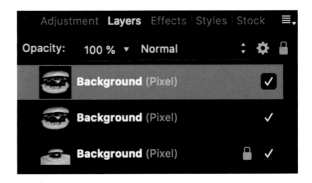

This is what the Layers Panel should look like now.

Select the **Perspective Tool** to *distort* the **top layer** of the hamburger. A pop-out window will appear.

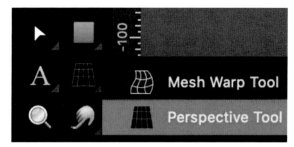

Click on **Show** Grid after the Perspective Tool's pop-out window appears. This will make the next step easier to visualize what we are about to do.

Click & *drag* on the **top two corners** of the tool and *place* the **duplicated hamburger** where you think its shadow should go.

Press **Apply** to close the Perspective Tool's pop-out window.

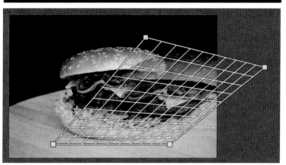

Move the **distorted top layer** and *place* it **above** the bottom layer so that its new position in the middle.

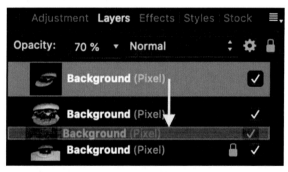

Make sure this is what you are seeing when you look at your image. If it's not, then you forgot to *press* **Apply** to the Perspective Tool's edit two steps above.

Make sure the middle layer is selected and highlighted in blue before continuing.

Go to the **icons bar** and *click* on **Add Pixel Layer icon**.

Go to the **Tools** and *select* the **Gradient Tool**.

Click & *drag* a **gradient** from the top-right of the distorted cheeseburger to the middle bottom of the original cheeseburger.

Go to the **Colors studio** and *click* on the **black circle** (see yellow square). This will make the bottom gradient node black. Ignore if yours already is black.

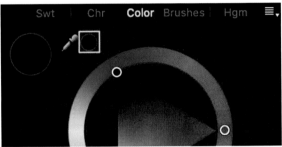

We can do this because when we created a gradient with our burger image (see image above) the gray node was selected. We know this simply because it's bigger than the white node. Because it was selected, just by pressing on this black circle marked with a yellow square, it changes the gray nodes color to black.

The result is the gradient goes from **white** to **black** (see this image).

Now that we have the gradient where we want it, we need to *move* the **Pixel layer** below-and-to-the-right of the layer currently beneath it - making it a child layer.

This will make the Pixel layer to be only applied to the middle hamburger layer.

Click & *drag* the **Pixel layer** below-and-to-the-right of the layer beneath it (see the yellow arrow for action).

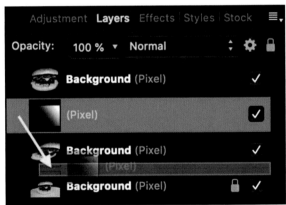

Select the **grouped layer** (see its circled triangle icon - not marked) and make sure it's highlighted in blue. This is what happens to a layer when you create a child layer - a layer that's below-and-to-the-right of its parent layer.

Important! Your Layers Panel should look like this now. If it doesn't, then this tutorial won't work. To close a grouped layer, just *click* on the **group icon** (circled triangle on the layer's left side).

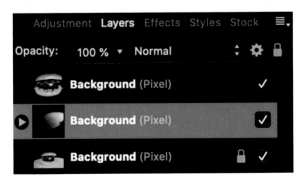

Change its **Blend Mode** from **Normal** to **Multiply**.

Our burger shadow is looking pretty good. The edges of the shadow do seem too sharp, though. So, let's correct this.

Let's add some needed blur to the shadow make it look more realistic. Make sure the middle-grouped layer is selected and highlighted in blue before we start:

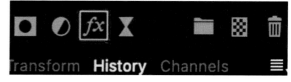

Go to the **icons bar** and *click* on the **FX icon** and a pop-out window will appear.

Select **Gaussian Blur** from the list of choices - it should be the first option.

Adjust its **slider** so its value box reads **7 px**. You can also *click* inside its **value box** and *type* **7** and then *press* the **Return key**.

Click on the **red X button** to *close* out **the Live Gaussian Blur pop-out window**.

Click on the **grouped layer** so it's active. When you do this **both** grouped layers need to be highlighted.

Select the **Move Tool** (or *press* **V**) to *reposition* the **shadow** if you'd like it in another position. We moved our shadow to the back just a bit so the shadow can't be seen in front of the burger.

Change the **Opacity** to **65%** to *reduce* the **strength of the shadow**. Changing the Opacity has a lot to do with the subject's surrounding and the overall lighting in the image. Try quickly typing **6, 5** to make 65%.

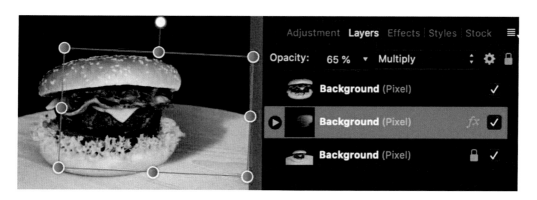

Done. This is our final image with its beautifully created realistic shadow.

Self-Quiz

What is the shortcut for doing these operations?

1. Undo
2. Print
3. Create a New Document
4. Paste
5. Copy
6. Duplicate
7. Group a layer
8. Invert
9. Open
10. Close
11. Save
12. Zoom in
13. Zoom out
14. Changing a Mode
15. Change Opacity of an active layer

Answers: 1-11 Start with **Ctrl/Cmd+** and their answers will only include the letter that follows.

1. Z
2. P
3. N
4. V
5. C
6. J
7. G
8. I
9. O
10. W
11. S
12. Ctrl/Cmd +
13. Ctrl/Cmd -
14. Hold down Opt/Alt
15. Type number 0-9

Finished. This ends this tutorial.

Tutorial 15: How to Make a Transparent Clothing Effect

Here's another creative technique where we'll show you how to take an image of man wearing a shirt and then placing his image on a road and then make his shirt transparent so you can see through him. This is a fun and interesting tutorial and we hope you like it. Later, you can use this same technique to make anything transparent and that skill could have many possible applications.

The two images we'll be using for this lesson are titled **Tutorial 15 - Man** & **Tutorial 15 - Road**. Here are the current hyperlinks to the images:

https://pixabay.com/photos/t-shirt-red-man-plain-model-1710578/

https://pixabay.com/photos/road-red-rocks-rock-formations-1303617/

Please have the image of the man in the red shirt in front of you so we can begin...

Go to the **Tools** and *select* the **Selection Brush Tool**.

Paint a **selection** over the white area around the man. You will have to make individual selections around his fingers, between his legs and up on his sides. To do this, make the Selection Brush's Width very small so it fits into these areas. Take your time and go the best job you can do.

Press **Ctrl/Cmd+Shift+I** to *invert* the **pixel selection** <u>onto the man</u> and <u>off the sides of the image</u>.

Go to the **icons bar** and *click* on the **mask** icon. Do you remember what will happen when we do this? The white background will disappear and be replaced with what you see in this image, the grey-white checkered background.

Press **Ctrl/Cmd+D** to *deselect* the **dancing ants** (the selection).

The second step we need to do is to *copy* this **image** & *paste* **it** on top of the image of the road. We've done this at least three times by now, so you should know how to do it. So, please do that now.

After you've copy/pasted the image on top of the road image...

Select the **Move Tool** (or *press* **V**) and *move* the **man** to the middle of the road (see this image for what we mean).

The third step is to make a selection of the T-Shirt to start the process of making it transparent.

Go to the **Tools** and *select* the **Selection Brush Tool**.

Make a **selection** of just the red **T-shirt**.

Go to the **Contextual Toolbar** and *change* the **Width** to make selecting the shirt easiest. You decide how wide you want to make it. If you have a QWERTY keyboard, you can use the left & right bracket keys to shrink or enlarge all brush tools.

Try to make your selection look like this image. We've done several selections together, so hopefully this selection will be somewhat easy for you.

Optional: Use the Refine... button's adjustment if you would like to refine your selection. We won't use it ourselves because the software has done a good enough selection.

If your selection looks good, *press* **Ctrl/Cmd+B** to bring up the **Grow/Shrink Selection** pop-out window.

In this pop-out, we want to adjust the **Radius** to **1 px**. This will cause the dancing ants to extend out 1 pixel away from the T-shirt.

Press **Apply** when done.

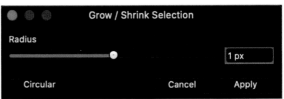

Press **Ctrl/Cmd+J** to *duplicate* the **man's lay**er. Check out what our Layers Panel should look like now.

Turn off the **top layer** by *unchecking* the **layer** (see yellow square).

Click on the **middle T-shirt layer** so it's highlighted in blue (not pictured here).

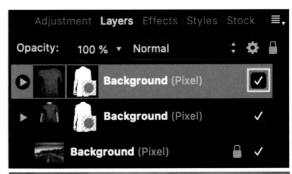

Go to the **icons bar** and *click* on the **mask icon**. After you do that, this is what our image should look like now. But this is the exact opposite of what we want.

To fix this:

Press **Ctrl/Cmd+D** to *deselect* the **dancing ants**.

Click on the **mask layer's preview thumbnail** located on the second mask layer on the current layer we are working on (see yellow square).

Press **Ctrl/Cmd+I** to *invert* this **layer**.

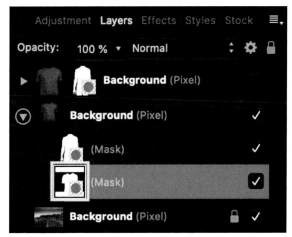

Important: Make sure you click on the layer and have it highlighted in blue before you invert it.

This is the image you should have on your canvas:

Note: A quick note about precision. If you look at the waist area of the man in the image we just worked on, you'll see a tiny white vertical line. We don't like seeing this. To correct it, simply zoom into the image and lines like these will disappear. If not, you can use the Erase Brush Tool (looks like the eraser-end of an old pencil) and erase away these annoying lines.

Let's now look at the Layers Panel and *activate* the **layer** that is currently unchecked. Remember to activate a layer we need to do more than click on it, we need to click on its checkmark so that it becomes visible again.

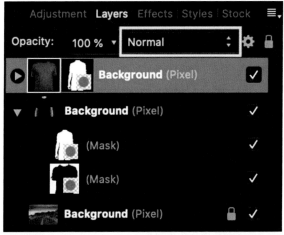

With the top layer active and visible, *click* on its **Blend Mode** (see yellow rectangle) & *change* it from **Normal** to **Overlay**.

Click on the **top layer's group icon** to reveal its two layers. Don't forget to do this.

We can now see the background behind the T-shirt, but it's still red.

To fix this:

Go to the **icons bar** and *click* on the **Adjustments icon** & *select* **HSL**.

Move the **Saturation Shift** slider all the way to the left (see yellow rectangle in the image below).

Press the **red X** in the top-left corner to *close* the **HSL pop-out window** when done.

This is how your image should look like now (we placed our image next to the HSL window).

You can see now that the HSL adjustment is affecting our entire image. This isn't what we want. We need to make it so that this HSL adjustment affects just the shirt.

Question: Do you know what a layer is called when it only affects its parent layer? It's called a child layer.

Let's make a child layer so the HSL adjustment layer only affects the top Background layer.

Move the **HSL Shift Adjustment** layer in the Layers Panel underneath-and-to-the-right of the top Background layer (see red arrow for this action).

Movement of the HSL layer:

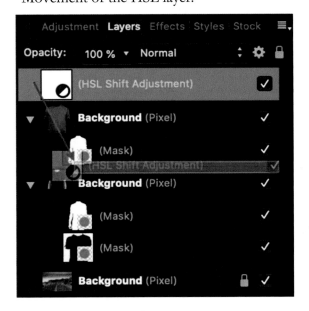

What our Layers Panel should look like now:

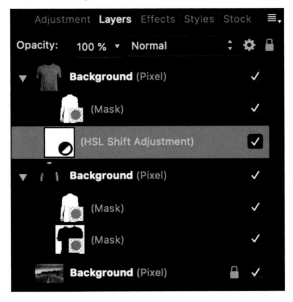

What our image should look like now. Our effect is almost done, but let's make the man's T-shirt a little more visible at the top.

To do this we're going to *apply* a **Levels adjustment**.

Go to the **icons bar** and *click* on the **Adjustments icon** and then *select* **Levels...**

Increase the **Black Level** to **13%**.

Click on the **red button** to *close* this **window**.

If you look at the shirt, you'll notice that it is definitely darker, but the road inside the shirt area is also darker. This darkening of the road isn't what we want. Here's how we'll correct this:

Select the **Paint Brush Tool** (or *press* **B**).

Set the **Foreground** color to **Black** to *reveal* the **road layer** beneath this new adjustment (see both sides of the man to see the color of road we're after here.

Go to the **Contextual Toolbar** and *set* the **Opacity, Flow**, and **Hardness** all to **100%**.

Paint over the **road inside the man's shirt area** to *correct* the **color of the road**.

Note: There are three primary ways to change the Foreground colors:

1. *Press* the **X** key to *alternate* between **Fore-/Background colors**.

2. *Go* to the **Colors Studio** & *click* on the **Black** circle to make it the Foreground color (yellow square).

3. *Go* to the **lower portion** of the Toolbar & *click* on the **Black circle** to make it the Foreground color (this only works if there are two columns of Tools).

Pro Tip: If you have different colors other than Black & White as the Fore-/Background, you can *press* the **D** key to instantly make the Fore-/Background colors Black & White and then simply *press* **X** to *switch* the **color** to your choosing.

Check out this screenshot of our work. We are partway done and you can see the area of the road we've painted over and the area we still have to paint. When you do this yourself, make sure not to paint above the height of the road.

We've added a crude yellow border for you to see where you need to not paint above. Do you see this yellow line? It runs between the man's two arms.

Continue painting over the rest of the road and when done, we are finished with this tutorial.

Here is what our final Layers Panel should look like:

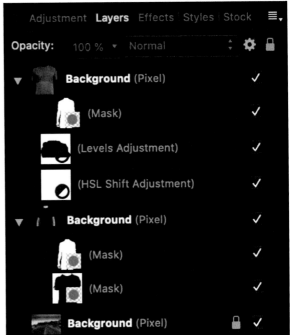

Done. This is our final image.

Finished. This ends this tutorial.

Tutorial 16: How to Put a Face on the Moon

This tutorial is just fun. It's the kind of effect families like to create with their children, parents, and pets. Who doesn't think putting real faces on other things isn't comical? We thought you'd like to learn this technique, so here it is. The images we'll be using for this lesson are named **Tutorial 16 - Face** & **- Moon**. Here are the current hyperlinks:

https://pixabay.com/photos/people-portrait-man-male-smile-1690965/

https://pixabay.com/photos/astronomy-full-moon-luna-moon-1869760/

Please upload both images and have the image of the man in front of you so we can start. The first thing we need to do is to make a selection of the man's face.

To do this:

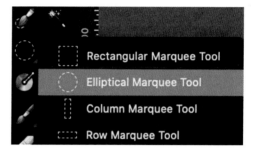

Go to the **Tools** and *select* the **Elliptical Marquee Tool**. You may need to click & hold on the Rectangle Marquee Tool if it's showing.

Position your **cursor** <u>over the man's nose</u> and then while *holding down* the **Shift+Ctrl/Cmd keys** *click* & *drag* out a **circle** on the man's face. The Shift key creates a uniformly round circle while the Ctrl/Cmd key creates the circle from the center point.

Go to the **Contextual Toolbar** and *click* on **Refine...** Inside this pop-out window, all we're going to do is *move* the **Feather slider** <u>all the way to the right to 100%</u> - just like how we did it in Tutorial 12.

Notice how the red Matte color is not clearly defined around the man's face. This is what feathering does when we refine our circular selection around the man's face.

Press **Apply** when done.

Next, we'll add the cut-out image of the man's face and place on top of the moon image/layer.

Press **Ctrl/Cmd+C** to *copy* the **man's face**.

Click on the **image of the Moon** at the top of the canvas.

Press **Ctrl/Cmd+V** to *paste* the **image** of the man's face on top of the image of the moon.

Select the **Move Tool** (or *press* **V**) & *position* the **face** in the middle of the moon. Try to get your image to look like this.

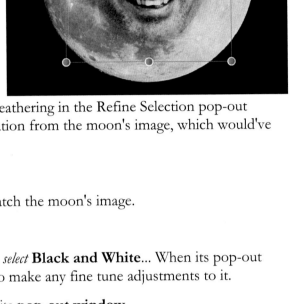

Note: Every time you use the Move Tool, these blue nodes that surround the face will appear if the image's layer in the Layers Panel is highlighted in blue. Once you click on the canvas around-and-not-touching our image, you'll see that the blue nodes disappear and the previously highlighted layer will no longer be highlighted (or active).

Also, check out the border of the man's face. Here you can see the feathering effect very well. The edges of the man's face are not distinct but blurred. If we had not adjusted the Feathering in the Refine Selection pop-out window, then the man's face would have a very distinct separation from the moon's image, which would've killed this effect.

The next step is to make the man's face black and white to match the moon's image.

To do this:

Go to the **icons bar** and *click* on the **Adjustments icon** and *select* **Black and White...** When its pop-out window appears, we'll simply close it because we don't want to make any fine tune adjustments to it.

Click on the **red button** in the top-left corner to *close* out of its **pop-out window**.

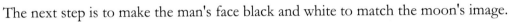

Note: Because the Black & White adjustment layer is located at the top of the Layers Panel, all layers beneath it will be in Black and White.

The next step we want to do is to blend the image of the man's face into the image of the moon so it'll look like they are more naturally melded together.

To do this:

Go to the **Layers Panel** and *click* on the **middle layer** so it's active and highlighted in blue (not pictured).

Change its **Blend Mode** from **Normal** to **Overlay**.

Press **Ctrl/Cmd+J** to *duplicate* this **layer**. When you do this, a new Background layer will appear above the layer you just duplicated. This image is showing the newly duplicated layer and it's active because it's highlighted in blue.

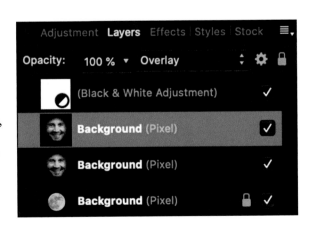

Did you know: Duplicating layers doubles the effect that layer had on the other layers in the Layers Panel and in our image on the canvas.

Change this duplicated layer's **Blend Mode** from **Overlay** to **Multiply**.

Hold-down the **Shift key** and *click* on **both middle layers** of the man's face. This will make both layers highlighted in blue.

Press **Ctrl/Cmd+G** to *group* them together.

After you do the above actions, this is what your Layers Panel should look like:

Do you remember the symbol for grouped layers? It's the circled triangle on the left side of the middle layer (see this image here). If you click on this circled triangle, the grouped layers will reveal themselves.

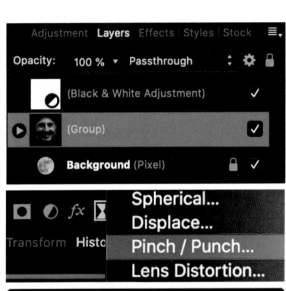

Right now, the man's face is a little too flat, so we're going to round it a bit.

To do this:

Click on the **Live Filters icon** (see partial yellow square).

Select **Pinch/Punch Filter**.

Increase the **Pinch/Punch** to **20**.

Bring the **Radius** up to **300**. Watch the image distort the higher you go.

Click on the **red button** to *close* this **window**.

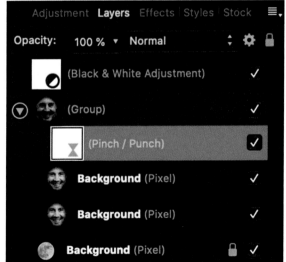

Now the face on the moon looks a little bit more rounded, as if it were actually on the moon.

Before we reveal the final image, let's take a look at our Layers Panel. This is what yours should look like now. If you want to go back and make changes to the Live Pinch/Punch effect, simply double-click on the preview thumbnail (just the white square) of the (Pinch/Punch) layer.

Done. This is our final image.

Finished. This ends this tutorial.

Questions

1. What's the difference between a Live Filter and a regular Filter?

2. When you duplicate an image's layer, where is the duplicated image located at?

3. When you use an adjustment layer and duplicate it, what does duplicating it do?

4. What effect did the pinch/pull filter have on our final image?

5. Which tutorial in this book has been your favorite and why? Send us your answer at kuhlmanpublishing@yahoo.com

Answers: 1) Live Filters are non-destructive. 2) Exactly underneath the source image on your screen. 3) Doubles the effect's intensity. 4) it makes the subject distorted towards you, the looker.

Tutorial 17: How to Create a Cool Transparent Text Effect

Here is the webpage for the background image we will be using for this tutorial. Feel free to use any image you want.

https://cdn.pixabay.com/photo/2016/11/29/04/19/beach-1867285_1280.jpg

Before we start, here is what we will create with this effect. We chose this image of the water to signify our beautiful planet Earth and how precious it is for all of us. We hope you like this tutorial.

Please follow along by doing each of these steps now. We've already covered how to do them, so now it's go time.

Upload your **image** onto the Affinity Photo canvas.

Select the **Artistic Text Tool** (or use the shortcut **T**).

Change the **Font** to **Impact** (or Arial Black).

Create your first letter on the left side of the image.

Type your all **CAPS word (EARTH)**.

Change **font size** to **1/3** the vertical size of the image's height.

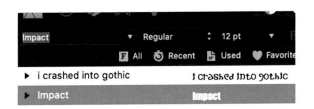

Select the **Move Tool** (or *press* **V**) & *move* the **word** in the middle of the image as well as use the **blue** dots that surround the text to expand the word to fit both sides of the image.

Note: Play around with the **blue** dots and try to make your text the same size and position as our text.

Once we had our word 1/3 the size of the image, we used the left and right nodes (not the corners) to expand the word to the edges of the photograph.

Note: If you hold-down the Shift key while you click & drag any of the four corner blue nodes, you can dramatically increase/decrease the scale of the word.

The next step is to create a colored outline around the text. You need to visualize the individual letters being transparent as in the image on the previous page. We are saying this because if we place a **black** outline on the text, we won't see it. So, for the sake of this tutorial, we'll first create a **white** border and then convert the blackness of the text to a transparent effect and then we'll add the **black** outline.

Ready?

Click on the **tab** labelled **Effects** (see yellow rectangle).

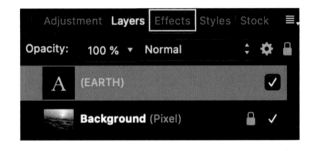

Check the option **Outline**.

In the pop-out window, there are a couple options:

Color - This is the color of the outline.

Opacity - This is the visibility of the outline color.

Radius - This is the thickness of the outline color.

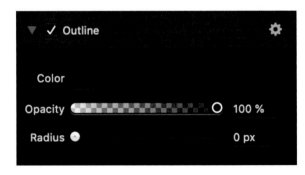

The first thing we want to **adjust** is the color.

Click on the **black rectangle** next to where it says Color and the Color Wheel will pop up (look at the previous image for the black rectangle - in the image to the right it's now white).

Move the **inside node** to where the color is **white** (see arrow for this action).

Close the **Color Wheel** pop-out by *clicking* on the color square again.

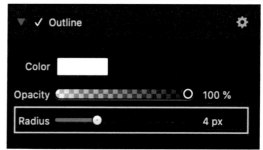

Move the **Radius slider** to **4 px**. This will create the white border around our text we want.

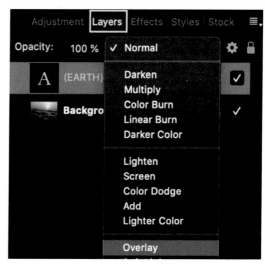

Now, we need to *change* the **Blend Mode** to create the transparent text effect.

Click on the **Layers tab** (see the yellow rectangle) so the Layers Panel reappears.

Change the **Blend Mode** from **Normal** to **Overlay**. The Blend Modes drop-down menu is immediately to the right of the Opacity value and below the Effects tab.

Our effect is almost done. If you like the **white** border on the text, then you're finished. But, if you want to see how to add the black outline, we'll show you on the next page. To quickly open the **Effects** (*fx*) pop-out window on our text layer, all we have to do is to *click* one-time on the *fx* **symbol** on the Text layer (see yellow square).

Hint: Knowing how to quickly pull-up previously used pop-out windows is a huge shortcut

Whenever you create any kind of adjustment or mask, simply *click* (or *double-click*) on that **layer's icon** (or preview thumbnail) and the pop-out window for that adjustment (or mask) will pop up.

Here is the **Effects** pop-out window. All you have to do here is to *click* on the Color square and change the color from **white** to **black** (see yellow arrow showing you the action of how to change the color from white to black).

Press **Close** when done - located in the lower right corner of this pop-out window.

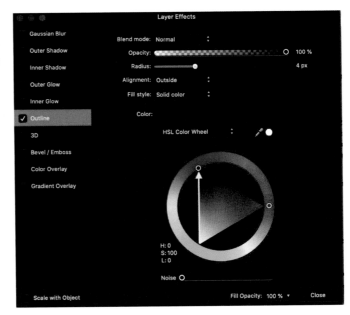

We're almost finished. To move the text around (up or down) on the image, *select* the **Move Tool** (or *press* **V**) to *reposition* your **text** wherever you want. We raised our text a bit higher than the mid-point.

Finished. This ends this tutorial.

Tutorial 18: How to Restore Old Photographs

Ever looked at old photographs and wondered if you could make them look "newer" or better without all their creases, rips & tears? If so, then this lesson is for you. We will look at a few ways you can make improvements to your old photographs without sending them off to an expensive photo nerd for professional work. The name of the image we'll be using for this lesson is **Tutorial 18 - Photo**. Please have it uploaded to your screen now. If you don't have a Facebook account, you may not be able to use the following hyperlink. If that's the case, we have the photo. Email us at kuhlmanpublishing@yahoo.com and we'll send it to you. Here's the hyperlink:

https://www.facebook.com/WritePublish/photos/a.351772392040734/1136819163536049

Let's begin,

Press **Ctrl/Cmd+J** to *duplicate* the **image's layer**.

Go to the **icons bar** and *click* on the **Adjustments icon** & *select* **Levels**...

When its pop-out window appears, make these adjustments:

Adjust the **Black Level** to **10%** & the **White Level** to **85%**.

Press the **red button** to *exit* from this **pop-out window**.

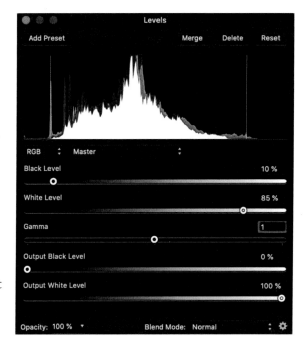

Some parts of the image have smudges & tears that we need to fix. We'll be using different tools to fix these different problem areas. The first area we'll work on is in the top-right corner of the image.

Click on the **middle Background layer** so it's highlighted in blue.

Select the **Inpainting Brush Tool** and then go to the Contextual Toolbar and *set* the **Opacity** at **100%, Flow 50%, Hardness 0%**.

Paint in the **areas** shown in our image below. Notice how we didn't paint per se but *clicked* **circles** of the Inpainting Brush Tool. Using clicks of the mouse keeps the tool from doing unnecessary corrections. Take your time.

The next area we need to fix is the tear in the photo on the woman's right arm. To fix this, we'll use the Clone Brush Tool. Remember, with this Tool we set a reference point and then paint over the area we want to fix with the area represented by our chosen reference area.

Select the **Clone Brush Tool** (or *press* **S**) so it's activated.

Zoom in to the **image** by *pressing* **Ctrl/Cmd +** so the woman takes up most of our screen.

Go to the **Contextual Toolbar** & *set* the **Opacity** to 100%, **Flow** 100%, **Hardness** 0%.

Hold-down **Option/Alt** & *click* on the **woman's arm next to and below the tear**. Can you see the black cross? This is the reference point the Clone Brush Tool will use to copy over the damaged area.

Paint over the **tear area** but be careful to paint only <u>vertically up</u> (& <u>down</u> if necessary).

Use **Ctrl/Cmd+Z** to *undo* any **mistakes** and go back and try again. This tool simply takes practice to master. Take your time and do your best. You can do it!

Done. This is our final image.

Finished. This ends this tutorial.

Tutorial 19: How to Transform Any Image into a Pencil Drawing

Probably the most popular tutorial ever is this one where we transform a color photograph and turn it into a pencil drawing. If you've ever wanted to learn this technique, then now is your day. The name of the image we'll be using is named **Tutorial 19 - Bridge**. Please locate it in the image folder and have it uploaded to your screen now. If you prefer to use its hyperlink, here it is:

https://pixabay.com/photos/bridge-golden-gate-sea-sunset-1333645/

Ok, let's begin by opening the image we are going to use for this tutorial onto the Affinity Photo canvas.

Once you have the image uploaded, here's what we do to create this cool effect:

Press **Ctrl/Cmd+J** to *duplicate* the **image**.

Go to the **icons bar** and *click* on the **Adjustments icon** and *choose* **HSL...** This will cause its pop-out window to appear.

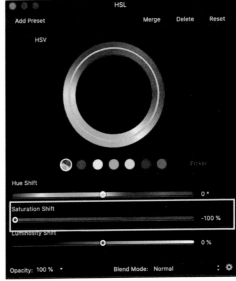

Bring the **Saturation Shift** all the way to the left to **-100%**.

Click on the **red button** to *close* the **window**.

Click on the **middle duplicate layer** so it's active and highlighted in blue.

Change its **Blend Mode** from **Normal** to **Color Dodge**.

Press **Ctrl/Cmd+I** to *invert* the **image** (or *go* to **Menu bar - Layer - Invert**).

When you do this, your image will become mostly <u>white and grainy</u>. Not to worry, we'll fix it next.

Go to the **icons bar** and *click* on the **Live Filters icon** and *select* **Gaussian Blur...** Do you remember which tutorial we did this exact same action?

Adjust the **Radius** to **0.9 px** to give it a sketch-like look.

Close this **pop-out window** by *clicking* on the **top left button** - when you hover your cursor over it, it should turn into a red X. If not, just click on it to close the window.

This is what your Layers Panel should look like. If your Gaussian Blur layer isn't highlighted in blue, it's ok. It doesn't need to be.

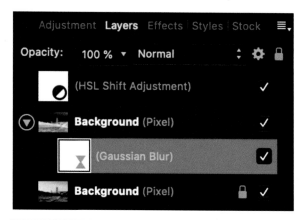

The last step in this technique is to adjust the **Levels** - this will add more contrast to our image.

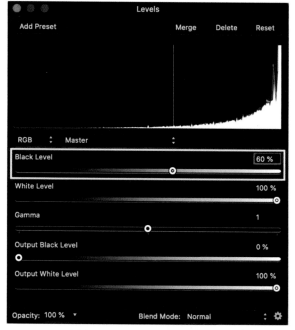

Go to the **icons bar** and *click* on the **Adjustments icon** and s*elect* **Levels**...

Adjust the **Black Level** to **60%**.

Press the **red button** to *close* this **pop-out window**.

Note: The higher the **Black Level** is the darker the whole image will become. If you were to increase it to **100%**, the whole image would be a solid **black**.

This is what our Layers Panel should look like now.

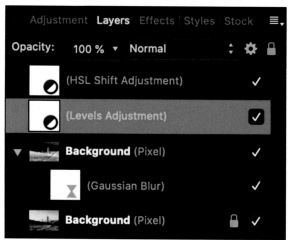

Done. This is the final image.

Practice

Find one or two of your own personal photographs and follow the same steps to transform your image into a pencil sketch.

Email us your work and in our next book we'll include your image(s) in our customer appreciation dedication. We'll pick the top four images to use in the book.

Might be fun.

Finished. This ends this tutorial.

Tutorial 20: How to Create a Jumping Over Text Effect

In this tutorial, we are going to learn how to make a jumping over text effect. It's a cool technique where use selections to create the illusion of text being behind the subject in our photo. The name of the image we'll be using for this lesson is **Tutorial 20 - Man**. Please have it uploaded to your screen now. If you don't have a Facebook account, you may not be able to use the following hyperlink. If that's the case, we have the photo. Email us at kuhlmanpublishing@yahoo.com and we'll send it to you. Here's the hyperlink:

https://www.facebook.com/WritePublish/photos/a.351772392040734/353071498577490

The first thing we need to do is to make a selection of the man's legs.

To do this:

Select the **Selection Brush Tool** (looks like a paint brush with a dotted circle around its tip). We've used this Tool several times so far in this book, so you should be familiar with it.

Go to the **Contextual Toolbar** and *adjust* the **Width** of the circular brush cursor so it fits within the inside of the man's pants (or more conveniently use the bracket keys on your keyboard).

Paint a **selection** on the legs (look at the below images to see what we mean).

Now, because we only want the selection on his forward leg, we need to remove part of the selection.

There are two ways to do this:

1. *Change* the **Mode** from **Add** to **Subtract** and *paint* over the **back leg-to-the-middle-of-his-belt-area**.

2. *Hold-down* the **Alt** button and *click* on the **parts of the selection you want to remove**. This is our preferred method as it's more intuitive and easier to do once you gain proficiency.

The image on the left is what our image should look like after we made a selection of the man's legs. The image on the right is what our image should look like now before we progress to the next step. Try to make your selection (i.e., the dancing ants) be in the same position as ours.

Now that we just have his leg selected:

Press **Ctrl/Cmd + J** to *duplicate* this **layer**.

Press **Ctrl/Cmd + D** to *deselect* the **dancing ants**.

Select the **Artistic Text Tool** (or *press* **T**).

Change the **Font** to **IMPACT** by either *typing* **"impact"** in the Font window (our image) or by scrolling down the massive list of Fonts until you find "Impact". If you don't have Impact, use Arial Black.

Type out the word **Affinity**.

This is what our image looks like now. If yours is different, you can use the Move Tool & reposition your text to look like ours. We've gone over how to use the Move Tool in earlier chapters, so we won't explain how to do it here. If you need help, turn to Tutorials 16 & 17 for review.

Ready to finish this lesson?

Click on the **top layer** so it's activated & *drag* it **beneath** the middle-duplicated Background layer in the Layers Panel (see yellow arrow for this action).

Note: Make sure the layer you move is not below-and-to-the-right of the middle Background layer. If that happens, *press* **Ctrl/Cmd+Z** to *undo* the **error** and try again.

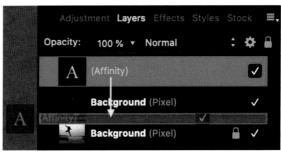

Done. This is our final image.

Practice: Please repeat this tutorial with your own personal images and place text behind and in front of your subjects. Practice doing this about five times so the steps will stick in your head

Finished. This ends this tutorial.

Thank you very much for going through this book and learning how to use Affinity Photo using our teaching methods.

If ever you need help using Affinity Photo, please contact us and we'll help you as fast as we can.

Bye!

Made in the USA
Las Vegas, NV
07 November 2024

11236337R10076